Opinion is really the lowest form of human knowledge: it requires no accountability or understanding.

The highest form of knowledge is empathy: it requires us to suspend our egos and live in another's world. It requires profound purpose larger than the self kind of understanding. "

 CENTRAL RIVERS
AREA EDUCATION AGENCY

Disrupt the Status Quo

www.codebreakeredu.com

DEDICATION

To the disrupters, the outliers, the outside the box thinkers…you're going to change the world.

THE
STATUS
QUO

INSPIRE. INNOVATE. LEAD. TEACH. LEARN.

BRIAN ASPINALL · DAPHNE MCMENEMY
MATTHEW X. JOSEPH · CHRISTINE RAVESI-WEINSTEIN

TABLE OF CONTENTS

INTRODUCTION

We are Brian Aspinall, Daphne McMenemy, Matthew X. Joseph, and Christine Ravesi-Weinstein. We are colleagues and friends. We met by chance. Four educators, four disruptors, looking for a place to fit in. The universe stepped in and we found one another. What you are reading is a book filled with first hand experiences and stories of both failure and success. We write about four critical topics important in today's educational environment – toxicity, failure, perspective, and voice – experienced throughout four different life journeys. Each section is divided by symbols denoting which author is writing. This is a book for every educator who, at one time or another, found themselves torn between following the norm and following their heart.

We followed our hearts and we wrote this book.

WHO ARE WE?

DAPHNE MCMENEMY

"I know people like you. You're a rule breaker."

I remember hearing this for the very first time some years into my career. It caught me off guard. I laughed, thinking the person saying it was kidding. I was met with a stare. They weren't kidding. And this wasn't a compliment.

It was something that really made me stop and think. Am I a rule breaker? No, I don't think so. I am many things. I am someone who questions policies and procedures that don't make sense to me but only because I want to understand. I can be a loud advocate for change and for what's best for our youngest learners. I have passionate beliefs about education that I'm not afraid to share with anyone willing to listen. And I ask for constructive feedback. I might even live in the gray in certain circumstances. The one thing I am not, however, is a rule breaker. In fact, I love rules. I follow the rules. I was the kid in elementary school who suffered from extreme anxiety when we had substitute teachers because I knew the rule breakers were going to give the poor soul a run for their money. I hated that feeling.

Younger me wasn't a big risk taker. She was afraid of many things. She liked safe choices. When my brother and I would walk to the bus stop every morning, I would beg him to walk to the crosswalk instead of crossing in the middle of the street (which felt like a six lane highway to six year old me, when in reality it was a barely busy street in an otherwise quiet neighborhood). Once in a while he'd oblige and we'd walk the extra five minutes down the road to the crosswalk. But this was only to shut me up, never to actually be safe.

Then there was the time we missed the school bus after school and I stood and sobbed while he held my hand and told me not to cry. In my head we were stranded and would never, ever see our parents again. I envisioned a dystopian nightmare where six year old me needed to prepare to battle the zombie apocalypse on my own. He and his friends somehow flagged down a city bus. The driver let us get on for free and dropped us off 10 houses away from home. I also remember someone on the bus with a radio playing *Girls* by The Beastie Boys while we all sang along. But that's a story for a much different book, likely titled *The Things You Shouldn't Expose Your Little Sister To*. But I digress. These memories are almost 40 years old and they're still fresh. They're fresh because breaking the rules and not doing what I was supposed to do was really stressful for younger me. It still is. You were supposed to cross at the crosswalk because it was dangerous to cross in the middle of the road. You were supposed to be on time for the bus so you didn't miss it. How else would you get home? I was raised believing that you did what you did because it's just what you're supposed to do. I didn't really question it. Not because I was afraid or wasn't allowed to. I just didn't think to. I didn't need to. I was safe this way.

I still happily live by many "supposed to's"; social conventions that are meant to be followed. But as my life unfolded, I evolved. When "supposed to's" become things we do because it's what has always been done, I'm not so willing to blindly follow along. There are so many "not supposed to's" in education. And too often we call the "not supposed to's", the "shouldn'ts", rules. But they're not rules. They're recommendations. Why? Well, because there's risk involved.

In many ways, I am exactly like younger me. I am as inquisitive and curious about random facts as I was when I was a kid. I am fueled by the creativity involved in making things, building things, and learning how things work. I think taking things apart is just as important as building physical robots. What's changed however, is how I approach the world, how I navigate it. I'm not as scared of life anymore. I'm not scared to question people. I'm not afraid to try new things. I'm not afraid to take risks. And I am a better person for it. More importantly, a better educator.

When "not supposed to" is thrown at me, I tend to clarify, "Are you saying I *can't*? or I *shouldn't*?" Then comes the look. The look that screams "I'm not impressed with your brazenness." But, there's a difference between can't and shouldn't. Why wouldn't I clarify? I've heard the word "shouldn't" so many times I've lost count. In my early days in the classroom, I questioned very little. If my administrator said it was so, then it was so. Over time, I began to question policies and procedures, rules and routines that I felt affected my students and the quality of education I was delivering. As I moved through my teaching career, I stopped being okay with the existing state of affairs; the status quo. I started questioning it more and more. Some saw that as disruptive, I saw it as necessary. If there is a way to do something better for our students, why shouldn't we? And that's when I was called a rule breaker.

I've learned that being innovative and thinking outside the box can make others uncomfortable. I used to believe it was because I was doing something wrong. It isn't. It's because I am doing something different. Taking risks and making change can make people see you as disruptive. Some may even go as far as seeing your disruption as anarchy or complete disorder: chaos. While chaos in the world brings uneasiness, it also brings the opportunity for strategic creativity and personal growth. Sometimes that disarray can be perceived as going against the norm. And when you go against the norm, it just might be perceived as breaking the rules.

MATTHEW X. JOSEPH

I vividly remember my first interview as a third grade teacher in 1995. I walked into the interview with a bin of student projects and artifacts I collected as a young teacher. The principal, two parents, and three teachers sat in the interview room waiting for my arrival. Remember, it was 1995, and a digital portfolio or website was not something widely used (sadly, it still isn't in interviews today).

I walked into the interview, took the blue top off my plastic bin, and proudly started showing student projects and lessons. I was so excited to share their work and thought there was no way I wouldn't get the job; who else would do this? Well, apparently no one; no one else would do this. The principal quickly ended my display, "This isn't show and tell, we only have 30 minutes for six questions, and we are already behind. No one brings stuff to an interview." My response? "Why not?" I wasn't being a smart ass; I honestly didn't know why you wouldn't bring student work to an interview. Needless to say, I didn't get the job and was very disappointed.

Sadly, for my following teacher interview, I caved to the norm and went into the interview with just my suit and a bottle of water. I answered the boring questions the exact same way I did in the last interview, and got the job.

What did this show me? It showed me that no one likes someone who thinks differently, so don't rock the boat. Looking back now, it wasn't that they didn't want someone who thought differently and brought student work samples, it's that the interview committee didn't know what to do with someone who broke the norm.

I was a good teacher, but I wasn't great. I planned units and projects and took a lot of field trips. My evaluations were always the same, "Mr. Joseph has great ideas, but kids are not learning the traditional way. This may hold students back in other grades. Also, his room is noisy compared to other teachers." The most common piece of feedback I received was, "I recommend you plan more traditional lessons so students are ready for the next grade." Oh, you mean bore them, so next year the teacher doesn't have to be creative? Got it.

Well, that feedback didn't sit well with me. So I said, *Screw it, I'll just be a principal.* I went back to school and earned my principal certification. But did I learn my lesson? Nope. I brought leadership examples from my internship and wrote entry plans for my first three principal interviews. How did I fare? You guessed it: 0-3. But I was fortunate to be offered another interview. I caved to the norm again, went into the interview with just a suit and bottle of water, and answered the dumb questions anyone who read *EdWeekly* could answer. I got the job.

I told myself after my experience that I would conduct interviews differently when I was a principal. I didn't want to ask traditional questions and I always requested student work samples. My superintendent even said, "That's not how you interview." But I did it anyway, and we got teachers who knew the job, had a personality, and had flexible thinking. I wanted to hire talent and someone with a growth mindset, not a robot who could read the curriculum and spout off buzz words. I always loved seeing the interviewees' faces when I would say, "Tell me your biggest pet peeve, so I don't do it."

Our school thrived. We had fun, and by our third year, we improved from 70% of all students meeting the state benchmark to 91.7% (yes, I still remember the actual percentage). We focused on adaptable thinking and celebrating attempts, not just the answers. And, of course, we had amazing teachers and supporting educators.

But did I learn? Nope. I was able to interview in a highly regarded district because of the successes of my first principalship. So what did

I do? I brought examples of our work including teacher evaluations (with no names) to show how I gave feedback. You guessed it; I didn't get the job and was told, "You scared the teachers on the committee with your energy and work samples." Seriously?

As it turned out, another opening in the same district opened up the following year, and the superintendent called me, "You are perfect for that school, but just show up, no props." *Props...oh, you mean samples of the work I would be doing?* So, again, I caved, and you guessed it...I went in with just a suit and bottle of water, answered the dumb questions, and got the job.

I have carried the memory of those interviews with me through my years as a principal and last seven as a district leader. I have learned that to make real growth, you have to move away from cheerleaders, toxic positivity, and people who always say "Everything is great." Instead, our students deserve educators who dare to be different.

Over the years, I've come to realize that you have to be different; focus on inspirational work. In short, you have to challenge the norm and disrupt the status quo. Sometimes this means taking the heat, standing alone on an idea, or leaving a job. Self-confidence is a trait we need in order to disrupt the status quo. The reason people stay in their lanes is because it's safe. It's safe to conform to the norm and go along with something even if you don't fully embrace it. I am not saying it's easy, and I admit to having conformed to the norm just to survive in a few districts; we all have. What I am saying is that it's worth doing, being who you are always is.

Disrupting the status quo is also true of my work outside of school districts. Take this project, for example. I am honored to work with three extraordinary leaders who are constantly disrupting the status quo; they are authentic in their work. I owe it to my co-authors and myself to be authentic in my writing. Moreover, I owe it to you, the readers, who often only see "all good" or "all smooth" tweets, photos, or text about our profession.

I've been in education since 1993. I've had ups, downs, more ups, harder downs, and so on. But I found real pride and success when I flourished or failed as myself. This is where growth lives and, in turn, where I found the most success for the students I taught or the staff in my buildings. I owe it to the profession to be authentic.

In August 2022, I delivered a keynote to kick off school in North Kingston, RI, USA. It was my best keynote because I made jokes, showed old photos, dropped a few curse words, and just had fun conversations with staff. They introduced me by saying, "Today, we have a wonderful speaker, Dr. Matthew Joseph." I took the microphone and said, "Thank you for that, I am honored to stand in front of you as a guy who has been in the field a long time and seen some shit, well, a lot of shit, and today I am going to share some stories and insight on how you can be unapologetically you and kick ass this year."

I write from the lens of a guy who brought work samples to an interview. The same guy who was given a briefcase after getting his first leadership job, only to never open it and carry a backpack instead (it's more comfortable and convenient). The same guy who wears baseball hats and golf shirts instead of suits.

Education is packed with unknowns, but over the past 30 years, I have learned that you can only control what you can control, and your ideas and thoughts matter. Trying something different is only different the first time; the second time you do it, it becomes your way.

CHRISTINE RAVESI-WEINSTEIN

TW: Mentions of sexual assault and suicide.

On August 12, 2021, I gave my first keynote address. It was the Code Breaker Summer Camp and it was a hybrid event. While I would be speaking live to participants at Whitman-Hanson High School in MA,

USA, the event would also be live streamed for those who were unable to make it to Massachusetts.

While my work with social-emotional learning and advocating for students with anxiety spanned two and a half years, and included two book deals, national speaking engagements, and numerous published articles, I had yet to take the stage to open a conference; I was scared to put myself out there.

I had no idea what I was going to say; the message I was going to give. I had 30 minutes to inspire people, empower them, and set them up for a worthwhile day of learning. I spent days worrying about what to do. I couldn't just get on stage and talk about strategies to support anxious students, that was effective for a concurrent session at a conference, not an opening keynote.

So I thought about who I was, what had gotten me to this point in my career. I wasn't being asked to deliver a keynote because I was successful at taking directives and analyzing spreadsheets during my day job as an Assistant Principal. Rather, I was being asked to give a keynote because of my willingness to be myself, to talk about who I was as a person, to lead with empathy, and have difficult discussions with people about real things: life, fears, and trauma.

Sure I could deliver a "professional" keynote. Much like I had mastered the game of school decades earlier, I had come to know how to be a professional, wear a label, and live behind the name on my office door. But there was nothing inspirational about the character I played during the day. From all the feedback I had gotten about the work I did outside of my office, I knew the best thing I had to offer was myself.

I stood on stage at the Code Breaker Summer Camp on August 12, 2021 and delivered my first keynote: "Disrupting the Status Quo." I flashed some professional accomplishments on the screen, but barely went over them. Instead I showed an abridged version of myself; a black and white selfie sitting at my desk in a striped shirt. I showed two pictures of my kids, each taken on a whim with no filters or photoshopping. I introduced myself as a 41 year old, divorced, single mother, homeowner, financially independent co-parent, living with anxiety and depression, and a survivor of childhood trauma, sexual assault, and a suicide attempt.

It was a risk to introduce myself atypically in a professional setting. It was unorthodox, surprising, and a disruption to the status quo. But what it wasn't was boring, familiar, and uninspiring.

I talked about authenticity and the need to stop trying to be perfect. I dove into social media and the filtered "reality" that drives our innermost self-depreciation and lack of confidence. I pushed attendees to think about what really mattered to them: "likes" or real connection? I asked them to rethink perfection and what a "perfect" day looked like to them. I encouraged them to disrupt the status quo by accepting that perfection is backwards, messy, controversial, risky, authentic, and truthful. And we do that, I explained, by being relevant, compassionate, and attentive to the stories of others.

The status quo is about perception. It's about presenting yourself as perfect; as someone who can withstand the toxicity life has to offer because we couldn't possibly be seen as a failure. We're expected to keep our opinion and voice to ourselves; disruptors might be shunned, or cast out of the social circle and what could be worse than that?

I'll tell you what's worse: living in a box, in the confines of unwritten rules determined by people more motivated by power or influence, or to be popular and attain "likes" than to inspire people to be the best versions of themselves.

People want to be connected. By nature, humans are social beings. But consistently, we fight the desire to be accepted, with the desire to be ourselves. By no means do I think I have it all figured out, but I constantly fight for my own perfection and believe that not only can everyone else do the same, but that if they do, our schools, our students, and our collective futures will be better for it.

So, on August 12, 2021, I told people to make the day perfect for them by taking a risk, being themselves not what's on a piece of paper, and letting the world know what they have to offer and why they're offering it. *This* is how you disrupt the status quo. *This* is how change happens. Being the first disruptor might be daunting, it might be risky to be in a camp all by yourself. But just like the question you're afraid to ask in class: if you're wondering it, so is someone else. Disruptors might start as solo venturers, but they'll soon be accompanied by more people, real people, perfectly imperfect people; the best kind there is.

Brian Aspinall

1100 1011

I really wanted my fourth grade teacher to like me. He carried a reputation for being tough and it was the first time I'd ever had a male teacher. He was an older man with a plethora of teaching experience under his belt, which excited me. I was eager to learn from him and challenged myself to be the best version of me. On Friday afternoons he would pass out word searches to the class as a weekly treat. I loved completing word searches. I was good at completing word searches. Damn good. This activity did come with a small twist, however. We were not allowed to begin until everyone had a copy and the timer was set. I always ensured my backup pencils were razor sharp in case of a casualty.

"Three, two, one, BEGIN!" he would shout as he clicked the bell. And the race was on. The scratching of pencils, coupled with the smell of fear and anxiety, made for quite the Friday afternoon treat. I was on fire and I was crushing it. I remember some students just doodling instead and I could never understand why they weren't participating. I mean, there is candy at the finish line. Let's go!

I used my own word search algorithm for efficiency. I didn't know it then, but my computational thinking skills gave me an advantage. If you found one word, quite often another one would exist perpendicular to it. Start at the perimeter. Explore the four walls of the grid of letters. Look for patterns. Debug. Repeat, row after row.

"DONE!" I would shout in a matter of minutes.

"Already?" Another student would ask, annoyed.

"Brian, bring it here," Mr. M said.

My outburst would always cause a stir. I imagine it made others frantic and I enjoyed every second of that experience. They were all looking at me. The doodler students would roll their eyes. They never received candy that year.

Mr. M didn't venture far from his desk very often. If we had questions, we were to form a queue and wait for our turn only to forget why we were there in the first place. Quite often I would return to my seat only to remember the question I had and place myself back at the end of the line, like walking in circles.

"Great job," he would tell me as he reassured what I already knew.

I was the king of the word search. I was the fastest word search completer in all the land. The community was talking about me. The world was talking about me. Well, in my head I figured they all were. I was breaking records in record time. I was word search famous!

Mr. M would give candy to the first handful of students to complete the word search with 100% accuracy, and I was always on the podium celebrating my accomplishments. Every Friday I would sweeten up on sugar for the long bus ride home with whatever goodies I was awarded that afternoon.

When I reflect on this experience today, I wonder what it might have felt like to be another student. How did it feel knowing you likely don't stand a chance against Brian Effing Aspinall?

Okay, I will put my word search completion ego aside and address the real issues here.

The reality of those Friday afternoons was that 90% of the class was already convinced they couldn't win long before the contest even started. And this contest measured speed and accuracy, something our math classrooms have celebrated for years. Sure, healthy competition can be a good thing, but not when it comes to academics, and especially at such a young age. We wonder why we experience math phobia with our students yet we place them in high stakes timed testing environments and tell them not to make mistakes.

But problem solving isn't always timely. And mistakes are bound to occur. In fact, the best learning takes place when things don't go as planned. When students learn to code, it almost never works correctly the first time, challenging us to redefine what it means to fail at school. How can we preach risk taking and embracing failure in a system in which failure is punished? Quite often, there is far too much risk in *not* getting the grade.

With the exception of math, I never typically graded students based on a quantity of correct answers. But why? Why is math assessment different? Is it a result of standardized testing? Why was I rewarding students with bonus points for showing up to gym class on time and prepared with a change of clothes? What message was I sending about grades in that subject area versus other ones? Imagine if I had given bonus points to students for coming to geometry class with their protractor sets. What a joke.

I think back to my word search title belt often. Am I providing an unsettling feeling at the beginning of math class for my students just like the Word Search Olympics? Do many of them already shudder knowing they need time to complete tasks? And by rushing, mistakes are bound to occur. Math cannot be scored based on a quantity of correct answers. Math isn't a score, golf is. And using grades as a reward or punishment system just reinforces compliance and trivializes any importance we think grades might have.

It's imperative we leave speed and accuracy to keyboarding skills, not mathematics. It is imperative we celebrate the process as well as the final product. It is imperative we promote risk taking and trial and error. As Seymour Papert famously said, "We need to create conditions for invention rather than provide ready-made knowledge."

In a world that changes overnight, the only strategy guaranteed to fail is *not* trying something new.

TOXICITY

"Whatever you do, stay away from her."

"Why?" I replied, but not with concern, that would have been mature. Rather, I strictly wanted to know so I could be a part of the water cooler conversations and accepted by my new colleagues.

Without ever having met this person, my mind was made up. I could have chosen any number of ways to respond, but instead, I made a mental note and was excited to meet her in person, just so I could add to the gossip in the staffroom.

I was a young teacher and green when it came to the social politics of a big staff. I'd come from a tiny school with less than half the number of colleagues and I didn't know a single person. I found myself quickly caught up in the clique mentality – that toxic culture wherein people see themselves as superior to others; where exclusion exists and group-think is rampant. Everything we teach our students not to do, I was right there in the middle of it.

I would learn over time that the people I was urged to stay away from weren't awful people, they were just different. For the most part, they were good people who tended to march to the beat of their own, very different, drums. I'd prematurely made up my mind about them based solely on the opinions of others. The thing about toxic social circles is that those in the circle don't see the toxicity. I didn't. It was a group of like-minded people who welcomed and wanted to be around others who were just like them. There's a fine line between a clique and a group of friends, and I skirted that line for a long time.

I would eventually realize that I had less in common with those colleagues than I initially believed. Personally and professionally we were quite different and that's when karma reared its ugly head. After a few years, I was the one being whispered about. I was the one who would enter a room to a sudden silence. I was the one wondering if the person talking to me was genuinely interested or if I was going to be a topic of conversation when I turned the corner at the end of the hall. But by now, the school had grown. I had grown. I had matured. I'd made a dozen new friends. My priorities changed. I learned to navigate social politics and be mindful of toxicity. I wasn't interested in the gossip. I had my very small circle and that was all I needed.

Over the next couple of years I was intensely focused on my career aspirations – on my classroom, my students, and my program. I was learning the ins and outs of the integration of technology at a time when technology integration lived in weekly visits to the computer lab. I was beginning to discover a world of education outside of the four walls of my classroom. I was intent on building a network I could access and learn from to help me build a program that could engage even the most hesitant of my very young learners. From the outside looking in, my ambition looked like it belonged to someone who was headed down the administration path and this was seen as problematic for some.

There are teachers who enter the profession having no desire to ever leave the classroom. There are those with their sights set on administration from the moment they pull into a school parking lot. And then there are those in the middle, the never say never group.

There exists a pocket of teachers in that first group that view the "climb" to administration as a negative thing.

I remember once chatting with a colleague. What started as a congratulatory conversation about a recent achievement of mine, ended with a snide, "Look at you! Climbing the corporate ladder!" To that, I replied, "Oh, I'm not climbing ladders, I'm building my own."

My ambition was somehow seen as problematic for others. It invited toxic comments which I almost always reply to with sarcasm. It became an unbecoming defense mechanism. Since then, I've worked very hard at not allowing toxicity to take up my energy. My silence is not a lack of a reply, it is the reply.

I walked away from that conversation wondering why we judge those who choose a different path than our own? But I know why. Because I am guilty of this type of toxic thinking, too. I'd be lying if I said it only came from a lack of understanding, but no, it also came from envy. I was envious of those who sought out goals that I believed I couldn't achieve.

While at this point I'd been teaching for a decade, I still felt like a first year teacher – like someone with still so much to learn. I hadn't really set my sights on anything bigger than what was in front of my face. But as my priorities shifted and new technology was entering the building, I began to see more opportunity; for myself and my students. It was cyclical. The more opportunities I had to learn, the more opportunities I could afford my students. Suddenly, the envy and judgement were gone. I was focused on my own growth and was celebrating my colleagues' achievements with genuine happiness.

When we fail to understand everyone's ideas or perspectives, we only see the world through our eyes. When we're not willing to see past our own objectives and push our insecurities aside, we get stuck in a pattern of thinking that won't allow us to fully appreciate what others bring to the table and how they arrived there. These kinds of environments are breeding grounds for toxicity.

I was beginning to build a bit of a reputation that would precede me in the years to come. Where I saw myself as an innovative, outside the box thinker who was learning to take calculated risks with curriculum delivery and student engagement, others saw me as a disruptor. This wasn't a good thing.

I was getting frustrated with the "that's how it's always been done" mindset, so I was finding new ways of doing the things we'd always done the same way. Some saw this as unnecessary, so there was pushback. I didn't understand the pushback. I saw the benefit of changing things. I was meeting my learners where they were. I was building stronger connections with student families. But rather than reflecting on, or considering their perspectives, I immediately pushed back on the pushback. Toxicity at its finest, even though I hadn't realized it at the time.

Some saw the changes I was making or advocating for as just a reason to be disruptive. This was a problem because my ideas weren't being heard by those outside my circle. It reached a point where they weren't even being considered – something I think was subconsciously decided before I'd even entered the room.

I was sitting in a meeting one afternoon with colleagues. We were meeting to talk about how the beginning of the school year would unfold. I was new to the team. I had a lot of ideas about how small changes could make a big difference for our learning community. But it felt like every time I spoke, everyone sat quietly. I was beginning to feel like this wasn't a discussion, but rather a list of what was going to happen, the way it had always been done.

The last time I spoke, my idea was immediately met with, "But this is what we've always done…as a team." It was at that moment it became very clear to me I wasn't part of the team. I began to resent these team meetings. They would only serve to remind me of the obvious: I didn't belong. And while I don't believe that was anyone's intent, I didn't have a voice, and impact always outweighs intent.

Toxicity exists everywhere. Sometimes it's loud and in your face, sometimes it's quiet and unassuming. But it's there. It's easy to get sucked in. And sometimes you don't even realize you're in it, until you're not.

I learned that breaking the cycle of toxicity means realizing that it's not actually about the toxic people we're surrounded by, but rather whether or not we allow ourselves to be driven by it. Toxicity in the workplace is dangerous. It can stifle growth, negatively impact communication between colleagues, and kill motivation. And if we let it, it can define who we are and who we will become. So, I surround myself with people who remind me to continuously reflect on me, on my choices, and my reasons for doing what I do the way I do it. With time comes reflection, and with reflection comes perspective and growth. This enables us to see our capabilities and reach beyond our potential. The toxic mindset is shattered when we learn to focus on the energy we're putting into our own personal growth and realize that the only ladders we need to climb are the ones we are building ourselves.

As an elementary school principal, I always strived to have a healthy and positive school culture. I wanted to see smiling faces walk through the doors on day one, the last day, and every day in between. I wanted this so much that I studied culture as part of my doctoral research at Boston College. But, even haven written a doctorate on culture, I'm still not an expert. In fact, anyone who says they are an expert in culture, actually doesn't know anything about it because culture shifts from building to building and community to community. What you do need to become an expert in is people. People follow people, not positions. To be part of a culture, you have to live, breathe, understand, and respect it, not just talk about it.

One constant about culture is that not everyone in the building or district is going to view culture similarly. Tom Hiddleston, the English actor who plays Loki in the Marvel Cinematic Universe, said, "Haters never win. I just think that's true about life because negative energy always costs in the end." That quote rings true in schools and corporations. And culture starts at the top. Yes, I said it. Culture begins with the leader. My two favorite movies are the original Karate Kid and the original Star Wars. Marvel Universe is a close third, so I had to give Loki a nod.

In the Karate Kid, Cobra Kai is a fictional karate dojo run by the badass, John Kreese. Kreese teaches his students to be merciless, and in turn, his students become intimidated by him and unethical. Johnny Lawrence is Kreese's star student; a self-centered, master manipulator. Lawrence is uncaring and unapologetic for the needs of anything outside of himself and the dojo. He is typically at the center of any plot or scheme designed to maintain control of his popularity or dominance in the group.

Now think of Star Wars. Even if you've never seen it, you know Darth Vader. Darth Vader was the Supreme Commander of the Imperial Force and led a large workforce of individuals. Whenever you hear the theme music as Darth Vader enters a

scene, you immediately get tense and nervous. How many of you have heard that same theme song in your head when your leader walks in?

You may be thinking, "Where is he going with this?" But let's look at the characteristics of both communities in these two movies:

- They have many followers.
- There is a strong leader.
- The followers are incredibly loyal, and others want to join.
- All members are convinced they're doing what is right.

Just because a group of people are in the same location, have a perceived goal, and are moving in the same direction, does not make the group positive. The Cobra Kai Dojo and the Imperial Force may be fictional (don't repeat that at Comic-Con), but if you reread the characteristics, you may see some similarities to a toxic school or district. The staff may be afraid to offer suggestions or ideas in toxic communities. In the fictional examples, the communities had a very selfish purpose, the norms did not change, and no one questioned the leader. Working to build a community where members are willing to try new things and feel supported creates a culture of risk takers. In my various roles in education, I often experienced the fear of being criticized in toxic cultures. It caused people to stay in their lanes. Sometimes, I wasn't willing to take the risk or challenge the status quo. A culture shift can change all that.

Toxic school cultures undermine improvement and kill motivation for students, staff, and leadership teams.

Before I could begin my journey to shift school cultures, I first had to identify the traits of a toxic culture. The following is a list of the common traits of toxic cultures I saw in my research and years as a principal and district leader:

- There is a lack of vision.
- Staff members blame the students for the lack of progress.
- Collaboration is discouraged.
- Hostile relationships exist between staff members and/or grade levels.

- There is a lack of communication from the administration.
- Policies and procedures are constantly changing.
- Expectations for staff members are unclear.
- Administrators are not accessible, which leads to a lack of trust in the system.
- There is no diversity among the staff.

Once I was able to define the characteristics of a toxic culture, my next step was a hard one. I had to look in the mirror and ask, "What aspects of our school culture are negative, harmful, and should be changed?" I recommend you do the same and most importantly, be honest. You have to be honest with yourself to make any real progress. If you answer, "None, we're great!" or "The staff is great!" or "Our school is great!" You are lying to yourself.

After I looked in the mirror and was honest with the shifts that needed to be made, I was ready to disrupt the existing culture. I told myself repeatedly that it takes time to shift culture and make change. Changing attitudes doesn't happen overnight. I knew the process of change started with me as the leader.

Early in my principalship, I thought being liked was the key to being a good leader. I quickly realized that toxic cultures often start when popularity is a priority. I needed to focus my time, energy, and initiatives on building respect for my work rather than being everyone's friend, i.e., the "popular principal."

I get it; it's inviting to make a popular decision your staff and parents might want or like. But I urge you to focus your decision-making on student needs. If you keep students' needs at the center of your decision-making, are consistent, and communicate "why"; the staff and parents will come to accept unpopular decisions. They may not like it, but they will respect it. Leadership is about doing what is right, not always what is popular.

As leaders, we must model the behavior we want to see in our staff and overall school culture. Even small actions like where or who you eat lunch with are opportunities to model behavior you would like to see in your staff. Eat with the students, spend time in the staff room, and be visible!

I also learned quickly that innovation in the building started with me. When I talked with teachers and encouraged them to try new teaching methods using the most recent technology, I knew I had to do the same. I even set up regular meetings to discuss new research on teaching methods or new edtech, and how these tools/strategies could be implemented in the school. I began using staff meetings as a chance to have technology showcases where the staff shared digital lessons. When I needed to learn new tools or techniques, I would go to a teacher who used them. This helped staff see me as a learner and build trust, two steps necessary in building a positive school culture.

I remember my days in the classroom when I would receive feedback from the administration. I often viewed it as a negative experience. I associated feedback with criticism. As a principal, while I used feedback as a means of evaluation, I also offered praise and a boost of confidence to my teachers. There was no need to be a "Snoopervisor." The "gotcha" mentality will get us nowhere.

I often tried to do everything as a principal but soon learned I couldn't. I was told, "If you want it done right, do it yourself." But that is not the case. Delegation will establish a relationship of trust with your staff and free up your time for other priorities.

In my first year as a principal, I also believed that a packed agenda was a sign of an impactful meeting. When I looked out at the blank faces, I realized that I was scheduling meetings for the sake of scheduling meetings. I could see the frustration on people's faces. Frustration can lead to toxicity. Shifting meetings from the dissemination of information that could have simply been put into an email to authentic learning opportunities made a world of difference.

These are just a few examples of how I went from a principal who followed the norm because it was easier and "it was how we always did it" to a principal who had the courage to disrupt the status quo for the best interest of the school and its students. I advise you to take a long, hard look at yourself and ensure that what you bring to the table is what you want to convey. Dare to be different and be the leader the kids need for a healthy community. Stop being the leader everyone likes. You may be creating a culture where people talk behind each other's back.

MY DARE TO BE DIFFERENT IDEA TO COMBAT TOXICITY

I love music, and when I was a principal I wanted to start each day listening to songs that put a smile on my face. So one year, for our PTO (Parent Teacher Organization) fundraiser, I said, "Let's use the money for outdoor speakers." Of course, my idea was met with, "That is not how we have historically used our funds; the PTO gets classroom supplies." I get it; the extra supplies are important. But I thought starting our day listening to music, smiling, and in a good mood trumped some extra markers. So I convinced the PTO to use the money for speakers.

In elementary schools, about 50% of the students are dropped off daily. Before the speakers and music, the kids got out of their car, heads down, and shuffled their feet into the building. It was not a fun way to start the day. The only staff outside were the ones assigned to drop-off duty.

Once we had the speakers and the music, I turned into the "Drop-off DJ." The kids jumped out of their cars, singing, high-fiving each other, and dancing. We even started a "request line," and kids made playlists. Furthermore, staff started to come out for drop-off even when they were not on duty.

The speakers and music created a welcoming environment that kids looked forward to. There were no morning arguments and no grumpy faces. Oh wait….a principal is supposed to effectively use data. How about this: our "on time" attendance went up by 12%, and we had under 7% tardy after the first two months and under 3% by the end of the first year. All because we played some music in the front of the building. In addition to the positive impact on students, the morning music changed the attitudes of the staff, too. Morning meetings were happier and more productive.

Enthusiasm is contagious and brings down toxic tendencies. When the kids were happy about coming to school, the staff were happy about coming to work. The staff even got into it, playing some oldies and educating the students about their favorite music.

To minimize toxic attitudes and improve culture, you must be an authentic and trustworthy leader. Music is my thing and it worked for me. If music isn't your thing, do what works for you. My good friend and leader, Dr. Chris Jones, is the principal of Whitman-Hanson High School in MA, USA. Every single Wednesday he makes inspirational signs to welcome his high school students to school. He is out in front of the school, taking photos and posting all the smiles and inspiration for others to see. You can follow Dr. Jones on Twitter at @DrCSJones to see the inspiration for yourself. Dr. Chris Jones is disrupting the status quo, are you?

Toxicity can evolve quickly without even knowing it. And once present, it can take years to change. People who continue to spread negativity or "fake positivity" are just looking to vent or gain something. If you are reading this book, let this be my final motivation to you to change your culture: You cannot be the person who walks into a room and has others hearing the Darth Vader theme song. Instead, be the leader who people give their music recommendations to, or better yet, their respect.

Note: Names, locations, and identifying characteristics have been changed to protect the privacy of those depicted.

"So, we don't have any more questions for you," the Assistant Superintendent explained, "but do you have any questions for us?"

I was sitting at a round table in the Superintendent's Office; it's July of 2022. I was in the middle of an interview for an Assistant Principal position at the district's high school: it was me, him, and the Assistant Superintendent who had just asked the question. We were in an otherwise empty District Office that sat above the town's middle school.

I had arrived at 3 p.m. that afternoon expecting to negotiate a contract, but instead found myself an hour into a formal interview with the district's two leaders. Fortunately, I went home after work and changed out of the shorts and t-shirt I had worn to work that day; summer schedules for administrators meant more casual office attire.

I chose to wear a jumper. The black legs emerged from the white top with black pinstripes just below my breasts. The jumper was sleeveless and low cut. The tattoos on my shoulders, biceps and forearms were all visible; even the one on my back peaked out from behind the material. While I went light on the jewelry, I did wear stud earrings, black pumps, and both of my smart watches. If I ever interviewed again, I told myself, I would do it as myself; no smoke, no mirrors.

"Well, I do have one question, although I'm not sure if it's a question so much as a statement," I explained.

"That's okay," the Assistant Superintendent reassured.

"As you know, this has been a very unorthodox process," I began. "I was interviewed via Zoom two days ago, and now I'm here meeting with the two of you. If I were to be offered this position, I would do so without ever meeting a building colleague in person, and without ever stepping foot in the building I would be working in."

"Yeah, this has been a very different kind of process," the Assistant Superintendent agreed.

"So, it's a little unnerving to think about that prospect. I don't know if there's anything you can say or do to alleviate those concerns," I asked.

"Well, if you would like," the Assistant Superintendent suggested, "I could arrange to take you on a tour of our new building with some faculty members if you think that would be helpful."

"I would love that," I confirmed.

"Okay, so we have some decisions to make, but if we were to move forward with you," she continued, "we would make some calls and be sure you had that opportunity."

"That would be great. Thank you. I also want to be completely upfront with you and say that while it's probably too premature to have this discussion, the salary is going to play a huge role in my decision to take a new job. I'm in a unique position in that I have a job and I'm happy enough in my current position, that it has to be the right move for me and my family to pick up and move."

"We completely get that," the Superintendent agreed, "and if we want to move forward, we wouldn't expect you to say yes to the position before such a conversation occurred."

"Okay, good. I really wanted to get that all out on the table before finishing up," I admitted. It was obvious at this juncture that my line of questioning was complete.

"Wonderful," expressed the Assistant Superintendent with an air of excitement in her voice. "So either way, whether we want to proceed with you as a candidate or not, I'll be in touch."

"Great," I said.

"Alright, let me walk you out," she said as she ushered me to the door.

As I got up from the table, I shook the Superintendent's hand and followed the Assistant Superintendent down the hall. Whether I got the job or not, I thought, at least I was myself; physically, and emotionally.

Prior to becoming an administrator, I spent 15 years in the classroom teaching science, more specifically biology. About halfway through my tenure teaching Advanced Placement Biology, the College Board changed the structure of the course. No longer was it about memorizing facts and processes. It was now designed around four overarching big ideas. The premise was for students to understand that every concept and topic we discussed could fit into one of four major themes in biology.

While inherently, the word biology refers to life and the processes that exist regardless of where an organism lives, there is a big idea that talks about systems interacting (via competition or cooperation) and the complexity of those interactions. No matter what biological systems we are born with, the systems we interact with outside of our own bodies will present complexities that will impact us, for better or for worse.

Of course I am simplifying this concept, but when it comes to schools, it's really no more difficult than this. Schools are an environment. Schools are complex. The interactions you have within your schools impact you emotionally, and in turn, physically. Like the concept of nature versus nurture, you can have the best intentions, disposition, and personality, but if you're not nurtured to be successful, not only won't you be, you will adhere to the same negative beliefs of the environment in which you work.

I ended up getting that job after the interview with the Superintendent and Assistant Superintendent, but not before I found myself in a negotiation that would give a used car salesman a run for his money. I was offered a contract at a number that didn't work for me. I countered with a higher number, a reach, and three days later I had a new gig and everything I asked for. Not only had I been myself in the interview, I had been given a private tour of their new building and a salary I needed. Could this be real?

Therein lies the problem: when you're treated the right way, you assume there must be a catch, something that makes it too good to be true. This is a long term negative effect of toxic environments; we grow to think they're normal. But toxic environments don't need to be, nor should they be, the norm.

Those 15 years in which I taught, I did so in the same school district. I ended up looking for a job elsewhere because I was convinced that school was the most toxic environment possible; cult-like. The professional incest I experienced there was real but it wasn't until I was cast out of the "cool kids club" that I came to see I didn't have to expose myself to it any more. I convinced myself that I needed to go somewhere else, get a fresh start, and be myself. What I didn't understand was that in my first district, the culture didn't ask me to hide who I was, it simply didn't care who I was.

So I applied to a different district. I was driven to be myself, take it or leave it. But from the start, my plan never took shape. Shortly after being named a finalist for the Assistant Principal position at the district's high school, I received a phone call from the school's principal:

"Hello?" I picked up skeptically.

"Hi, Christine?" questioned the voice on the other end.

"Yes, this is her," I confirmed.

"Hi, it's Peter Smith from Sunset High School."

"Hi, Peter."

I had no idea what Peter could possibly be calling me about. Perhaps the schedule for the finalist interviews changed? Maybe I needed to prepare something specific for the community?

"I'm going to give you some unsolicited advice," Peter opened.

Or, that, I thought.

"Okay," I replied. Clearly it wasn't a choice at this point.

"There is a picture of you on Facebook. You're in a sports bra and you're flexing. It's creating quite the stir here. You should remove the picture and check your privacy settings on your account," he suggested.

"Oh, okay," I replied, stunned at the request.

"Alright. Thanks," Peter said before ending the call.

The picture I was asked to remove from Facebook while interviewing for the Assistant Principal position.

As the line went dead, my heart started racing. *Facebook picture? Flexing? Privacy settings?* As I tried to comprehend the conversation, I signed into my Facebook account, searching for the picture in question. As I logged in, there it was; one of my five featured photographs. A picture of me in my garage flexing for the camera after an intense cross training workout.

An avid exerciser, I had been working with my sister, a former personal trainer, for almost two years to regain my health and confidence after my second child. I'd been working out (running and weight training) 3–5 times a week. I'd gone from 190lbs at the peak of my second pregnancy, to 150lbs. I was a mother, a wife, and an educator finding time to take back control of my life. It was a picture I was proud of. There was nothing sexual about it; everything was covered. In fact, it was less revealing than a picture of me in a bathing suit. "If I was a man," I told my friends and family, "Peter would never have called and asked me to remove it." Not a single person disagreed.

I thought about taking my name out of the mix for the Assistant Principal job, calling Peter back and saying, "I removed the picture, and also my name from your list of finalists." But I didn't. I complained about it, felt marginalized because of it, but didn't stand up for myself, for the proud, confident female I thought I was. Privacy settings intact, I hid behind the woman I was, just like my Facebook account now hid behind the reality of my existence as a strong, professional woman.

Cowardly, I moved forward with my final interview. I stood in front of the community, camera on, tempered make-up, tattoos covered, and spoke about the school community I wanted to be a part of like a sell-out.

I ended up being offered the job. Still unsettled about the blatant request to edit who I was, I reluctantly accepted. Sure, I finally landed an administrative job, something I had worked towards for four years, but it didn't feel right. It felt like I had to conform; be the administrator they wanted and not the administrator I wanted to be.

At the time, I could never have expressed my feelings as clearly as I can now. All I knew then was it didn't feel right because I was still bothered by Peter's request to remove my photograph. But I thought I could win them over; prove I was the right hire regardless. I walked into my new role on July 1, 2018 optimistic and eager to be myself.

But the request for me to remove my photograph was just the beginning. It was the teaser trailer for what would become a movie about my life at Sunset High School; me the protagonist, and Peter the antagonist.

Over the next four years, I slowly began to lose myself. While my professional career outside of the district took off (it was March of 2019 when I was first published in an education magazine), my work in the office became more and more disconnected to who I thought I was.

I was rumored to be having an inappropriate relationship with a district leader, sparked by a teacher seeing an interaction between us and reporting that I "might have been uncomfortable." Mind you, I wasn't uncomfortable and didn't report anything on my own.

The administrative team I was on was anything but a team. Made up of four, including myself, and another Assistant Principal, Peter and the Associate Principal, Kim, were inseparable and always plotting behind my back. Whether it was Kim reporting the apparent "affair" to Peter, telling him she didn't think I was a team player or working hard enough, or the two of them conniving to take my Administrative Assistant away from me and place her back into Kim's office (I inherited her from Kim when I got hired as Assistant Principal and she moved up to Associate Principal), I was just a soldier on the team; someone there to take direction and analyze spreadsheets. Kim even went so far as to tell me I didn't live up to her expectations when I was hired. After school I was a published author and nationally recognized speaker. But during school I was, to put it simply, a disappointment.

Nature versus nurture. On the one hand, I was being nurtured to be an impactful leader. Encouraged to engage in passionate conversations about my life, upbringing, anxiety and depression. On the other hand, I was nurtured to see myself as nothing more than a woman in a man's world. An emotional, inexperienced woman, who simply needed to keep her mouth shut and her nose down. In fact, by the time I left, the administrative team at Sunset High School had grown to five, four of whom were older white males and all alums.

Toxic environments are painful. What makes them so painful is not their mere existence (you'll find them everywhere), but that they'll quietly brainwash you to believe that:

1. You're the problem.
2. You aren't as good as you thought.
3. They don't really exist (they're just a figment of your overreaction).
4. Your experience is normal.
5. If you just work harder, you could change the narrative.

But the thing about toxic environments is they're like quicksand; the more you fight against their grip, the tighter they squeeze, and the less likely you are to ever get out. And just like quicksand, the only way you can get out, is to fight less. Sit quietly in the background, do what's asked of you, and when the opportunity presents itself, take the chance. Pour all of your energy into that one opportunity, that one window to escape; a more nurturing environment does exist.

I was offered the Assistant Principal position in the new district in the summer of 2022 after interviewing in my sleeveless jumper with the Superintendent and Assistant Superintendent. The Superintendent called less than a week after that meeting and offered me a contract; I declined. When asked what salary it would take to get me to accept, I quoted a price. Not sure he could meet my demands, the Superintendent asked for a couple of days to get creative and find me additional money. Less than three days later, he called back and offered me everything I asked for; no loopholes, no clauses, no underlying expectations, no questions asked.

Of course a higher salary is always nice; an incentive that can be hard to pass up. But the intangible the district offered was nothing monetary. Instead, what they offered was the clarity that toxic environments do exist, that they change who you think you are, and that they will, slowly, and decisively, eat away at you from the inside out. And if I thought not caring who I was, made for a toxic environment, asking to hide who I was even worse. For these reasons, and these reasons alone, there is no amount of money that should be worth more than seeing your environment for what it is; that's invaluable.

"Hey man, stop being so sensitive," he said.

With that statement, I hit the roof.

I love my community. I love my neighborhood. I love being surrounded by Lake Erie in all her beauty. She reminds me to never sit still. She pivots hourly and makes those who call her home, do the same. My hope is that my students one day will learn to pivot like that. I want them to see roadblocks as an opportunity, not a negative event.

In the summer of 2019, my wife and I made a decision to become vacation rental hosts. Our goal was to provide places and experiences for others to enjoy the Great Lakes. We wanted to support our local wine industry which hosts dozens upon dozens of weddings every summer season. However, we are more than 30 minutes from any major city. That means 30 minutes from any accommodations. While this proved to be problematic for the wedding and wine industries, it proved to be an opportunity for us. It provided a chance to pivot and to try something new. I had used vacation rental apps for my work travels countless times, but I had never been a vacation rental host before. I was about to embark on some huge learning.

We purchased a new cottage on Lake Erie in the fall of 2020. Due to the global pandemic, international borders were closed for the foreseeable future. I live in beautiful southern Ontario, Canada, a stone's throw from Detroit, Michigan. With the exchange rate close to 30%, there are a plethora of American owned cottages on Lake Erie's north shore as their dollar goes much further here.

But with the world being grounded, many Americans were forced to sell their cottages. This was a chance for us to make some strategic negotiations and take possession of many sought after properties.

This one in particular needed a ton of work. We knew it had been built in the 40s and it still looked like 1940 inside. We had a hunch it needed to be gutted to studs, but we had no idea it would also need new electrical throughout. At the time we took possession, we entered with our new keys, excited about another project.

"Why is the power off?" I wondered.

I headed to the panel, which had been updated. I learned in that moment a new panel was installed strategically for insurance, but nothing running to the panel had been updated. Someone was duped.

As I began to explore further, it became evident that the entire property still had knob and tube electrical wiring – something deemed very dangerous by today's standards. So much so that getting insurance is problematic. Luckily we were grandfathered 30 days to make the upgrade by our insurance company.

Electrical wiring is beyond my wheelhouse. Way beyond. I did some research, watched a ton of video content, and finally admitted to my wife that we should probably hire a team.
So we did.

A father and son duo from my community stepped up to the plate. I was familiar with them as I attended high school with a younger brother. Small town life. Everyone knows everyone. There are many pros and many cons to that.

I was happy with our choice. They seemed reasonably priced and assured us the job would be done in a timely manner. Though, as much as I asked for a deadline, they couldn't offer one.

"We will know more as we get started," they'd said.

This made me stop and consider my own university courses. This school year marks my eighteenth in education. After 12 years as a middle school teacher, I am now a University Instructor at a variety of faculties of education across Ontario.

Every course I instruct has deadlines. Obviously we have to keep everyone on pace as we work through the semester. But I often wonder what strict deadlines do for peoples' anxiety. Can we even assume each teacher candidate needs the same amount of time to complete each module? Why do we stop differentiating for adult learners?

After a few weeks of progress, I found myself on the hunt for receipts. They kept purchasing materials and invoicing me but I never saw the actual material list bills. It felt a bit shady to me but I never thought they would steal. I expressed my concern, after all, I need original receipts for Canada Revenue. If I flip a rental property for a profit, the profit becomes a taxed capital gain. You can use the receipts from work completed against that tax bill. I needed original receipts.

Immediately, they felt confronted.

That wasn't my intention. But I do recognize intentionality versus impact.

"I need original receipts for capital gains."

"We know what capital gains are," they replied.

Clearly they thought Teacher Brian was going to give them an education.

What was meant to be a brief chat quickly escalated and I found myself staring down a six foot five, 300lbs contractor who was ready to bash my head in with a two by four.

My limit came when one of them told me to keep my wife off Pinterest.

"Pardon me? This is her house too!"

"We have plenty of design ideas already."

"THIS IS HER HOUSE!" I shouted as I had yet to regulate myself and notice my emotions climbing.

What felt like an eternity was merely a few heated minutes. But it got hot fast.

"Hey man, stop being so sensitive," one of them said.

That was the last straw. We were done. Take your toxic masculinity and shove it.

I reflect on this experience often. I like to read a lot about the science of discipline versus punishment. When students are "in trouble" are they punished for it or does it become a teachable moment? Why do we operate classrooms and schools based on compliant fear? My classroom was always flat, meaning no hierarchy. I teach you. You teach you. You teach me. Every person in my school knows something I don't. That's beautiful when you really step back and look at the collection of experiences one building has.

Somewhere along the line, my contractor friends must have been taught that men can't be sensitive. As UFC fighter Paddy Pimblett recently said, "People would rather, I know I'd rather, have their mate cry on their shoulder than go to their funeral. So please, let's get rid of this stigma and men start talking."

Early on in my teaching career I had new kindergarten physical education classes to teach. These were also the days I cried on my way home from work. Kudos to every kindergarten educator out there. You are remarkable human beings. I remember some kindergarten educator friends trying to get students to stop crying. I was always puzzled as to why we never found the root cause of the tears, but rather tried to just make them go away. If we knew why they were crying, we could focus on that. And wouldn't that help prevent future tears?

I see a lot of toxic stuff on social media these days. After all the world has been through recently, I understand the intention behind certain posts. But I also question whether the content creator considers the impact on their audience.

Sometimes I just don't want to be joyful. And that is okay. Sometimes I want to be sad. And that is okay. Sometimes I want to be angry. And that is okay. Sometimes I want to cry. And that, too, is okay.

We are living in the most anxious of times. We are constantly bombarded with "thou shalts" and diet and exercise pills. We continuously read headlines about celebrities taking trips during lockdown and we continuously see the media spin it in such a way that we feel we are missing out on something. Clickbait sells newspapers. Clickbait improves video watch times. Catchy titles get clicks.

I get it. But do our students? Or do they take these things at face value?

Again, intentionality versus impact. Even our best intentions might negatively impact those around us. The key difference is whether we have open, honest, two-way lines of communication with those we serve.

If we are constantly preaching the joyous narrative, we are not only lying to ourselves, but also to our students. You don't get rainbows without rain. We need to help students regulate. We need them to try to understand their own emotions and feelings and dissect them. But we need a classroom community that is safe enough to allow this to happen. And that begins when the educator knows how to regulate themselves. I am guilty of hollering at students because of my mood. Some days you just bring home life to school. And so do our kids. I've come to learn that behavior is a form of communication and quite often the reason for it will make you sad, not angry.

Today my wife and I have one rental property in our portfolio. The global lockdown saw my keynote speaking and consulting opportunities come to an immediate stop. Things have improved since, but we are happy to no longer be vacation rental hosts. No hard feelings, just time to pivot again.

The other day I was cutting a hole in the brick wall of the house with my business partner. We were installing a patio door where there was once a window. As a result, I needed two sheets of plywood to cover the new hole while we waited for the patio door to arrive.

"Risk Taker!" the gentleman said as I approached the hardware store entrance. I was wearing a *Risk Taker* t-shirt, hence why he shouted this at me.

Sitting outside was a former neighbor and he was volunteering for a local event.

"Risk Taker!" I laughed. "The title of my third book."

"Three books? Wow!"

"Well, four now."

"Are you still at the university?" he asked.

"I am. In fact I'm writing a new technology course, too."

"And still doing real estate?"

"Not as much now that the world has reopened and I am allowed to travel for work."

"Keeping the wife happy?"

This was his final question. Not because we were at the end of his impromptu exam, but because I wasn't interested in continuing.

The wife. THE wife. Are you keeping THE wife happy?

What a ridiculous question. My job as a husband is not to keep her happy. My job as a husband is to worry about my own mental health and make sure we have honest, open communication. My job is most certainly not to keep her happy. That is her job and I am here to support however I can.

Admittedly though, when I heard the question, I panicked. At that moment I instinctively questioned my ability as a husband and whether Steph is happy.

If she wasn't, she'd tell me, I thought.

"Happy wife, happy life, right?"

I smiled and nodded and continued into the store.

Phrases like this have been passed around for decades. These kinds of phrases create expectations that are not only stereotypical but more often than not, unrealistic. Our job as educators isn't to keep kids happy. That will only frustrate us when we cannot make it happen. Our job is to listen and learn. To teach and explore.

Simply put, our job is to be a good person. We need to accept and understand. We need to teach and not punish. But most importantly, we need to be okay with not feeling okay. When we model that, we create a community of risk takers. A community of empathetic listeners. A community of people who won't hate someone else just for having a different opinion. When we model that, we create a community of people who learn that living above toxic cultures and mindsets is what allows us to grow.

FAILURE

"She thinks you hate her."

Those words stung. But I didn't show it.

"She thinks you hate her."

Those words hurt. But I refused to acknowledge my responsibility.

"She thinks you hate her."

Those words would change me. But I didn't know it in that moment.

In that moment I was offended. In that moment I chose defensiveness. In that moment I chose to negate everything this mother was telling me. She was upset and I was blaming her eight year old daughter for my actions.

It was early in my teaching career. There were days I thought I knew everything there was to know about teaching and there were days I very clearly had no idea what I was doing. Fifteen years later and that hasn't changed much. But I digress.

In this particular year, I was having a really difficult time making connections with some of my students. Actually, if I'm being honest, it was more than some. It was most. I wasn't experienced enough to know what they needed or how to reach them. And at some point, without even realizing, I'd stopped trying. Instead, I became the authoritarian teacher who, rather than striving to build any kind of positive relationships, made sure they knew I was the boss.

As you can imagine, this tactic didn't work any better. In fact, it usually made difficult days worse; much worse. Especially for one relationship in particular. No matter what I did, this one student just wouldn't listen to anything I said or asked of her. What I hadn't realized was that she was thinking the exact same thing about me. We would have loud power struggles. At what point did we decide that yelling at students was a means to control their behavior? I was in charge and would remind her of that. But she was eight years old and had full control over my emotions.

That same year I was taking an Additional Qualifications course – courses teachers take to upgrade and receive qualifications in various subject areas. I don't remember much about the course and by "much" I really mean, I can only remember one specific evening. I sat at a desk in a high school classroom with a notebook and a pen. I was likely doodling (because I knew everything already, remember?) when I realized our instructor was raising his voice. He was emotional, passionate. It got my attention. He was talking to us, a group of mostly new-to-the-profession teachers, about the importance of knowing our students.

"You know your students!" he started. "You know what buttons to push! You know how they'll react!"

I remember so clearly what came next. It was like he'd had a window into my classroom. He looked around the room, but I was certain he was only looking at me, and loudly followed with, "DON'T BE THE FUEL TO LIGHT THEIR FIRE!"

I don't remember what he said after that. I could only think about what was happening within the four walls of my classroom back at school. I'd reached a point in the year where I was so frustrated with this one student that I was almost welcoming the chaos; it gave me an excuse to send her to the principal's office. As I saw it, at least for a short while, she could be someone else's problem. But my instructor was right. I knew exactly what buttons to push. I knew exactly how she'd react. I wasn't only adding fuel to the fire, I was the fuel. And so almost every incident would eventually end with her walking out the door. I was showing her that I was in charge. I thought I was winning when in actuality, I was failing. I was failing myself. I was failing my students. But mostly, I was failing her.

The day after one particularly emotionally charged afternoon that ended with her in the principal's office and yet another phone call home, she wasn't at school. And then she wasn't at school the day after that. And then, a third absence.

During recess on that third day, I wandered down to the office and standing right there in the front foyer was her mother. I froze. She looked at me and asked if we could speak. My back was up. After all, I hadn't done anything wrong. That's what I was telling myself, anyway. We tucked into a conference room and she began.

"…I haven't been able to get her to school for three days…"

I nodded. I didn't know how else to respond.

"…She doesn't want to come to school anymore…"

I knew exactly why she didn't want to be at school. Why would she? I had made it a horrible place for her.

"She thinks you hate her."

Five words that I've carried with me since that day.

I couldn't tell you how the rest of the conversation went. I only know how I felt when it was over. I had failed this little girl. I had failed her mother as I stood there in that moment and deflected what was being said. No student, no parent or caregiver should ever feel this way. We have so much power in our profession to make good days great and bad days worse for the young people who sit before us. I chose to rule with an iron fist because I didn't know what else to do. And while I knew it wasn't a strategy that was working, I hadn't changed what I was doing.

Until the very next day.

I went home and realized I had to change what I was doing. A colleague once said, "You don't have to like all of your students, but they should never know that." I walked into the classroom the next day determined to repair the relationship I had destroyed before it even started. It took a long time. But I'd figured out that all I had to do was listen – to what she was saying, and what she wasn't. The only way to do that was through reflection.

You see the thing with failure is that when we learn from it, when we stop to reflect and make necessary changes to be better, we grow. That's not easy to do. We have to be willing to look inward, past our own intentions, and listen to harsh truths. We have to put ego aside and remember we are all human. We need to be comfortable with discomfort. After all, we got into this business to be a lifelong learner, right?

Midway through my career I was working with a new teaching partner. I was excited for the opportunity to share my ideas with my new partner and she was equally so. We were looking forward to collaborating and building a program together for our very young students. But I'd never shared a classroom before. I'd worked with other educators who spent a few periods a day in my classroom working with specific students, but that was the extent of it. Spending an entire day nearly side-by-side, working together to deliver one program to one group of students was a brand new experience for me.

Once the school year started, it became evident fairly quickly that we were very different people and not the good kind of different, the kind that compliments one another. Rather, we were two educators in one room with conflicting perspectives about some of the most important aspects of education.

Our relationship became one of co-existence. We weren't partners. And while I think we were both feeling the same way, I can't speak for her. I only know I was of the opinion that we couldn't see eye-to-eye and we couldn't agree on program delivery and classroom management strategies. Our partnership was a lost cause. And while that was factual on a surface level, what I came to realize later was that that only happened because we failed to see how our communication styles were being interpreted by the other person.

One evening after school, I walked into my administrator's office. I was so frustrated. I was venting. I was pacing. She sat and listened as I listed all the things I was doing right and how I just couldn't understand why my partner couldn't see things my way, the right way. I cringe when I say this now. "The right way." I was so focused on what I was doing right and what she was doing wrong that it never occured to me that perhaps there was something I wasn't seeing. When I finally took a breath, drained from another long day, I was ready to listen. She spoke softly, without judgement.

"Daphne…you ask a lot of questions."

"I know," I said. But I didn't know. I had no idea, actually.

"When I first got here, I remember you coming to me, asking a lot of questions."

I stared. I was worried. Where was this going? I wanted her to be on my side. That in itself was a huge problem. I was still thinking there were sides to take.

"It came across as you questioning me. Questioning my decisions – about everything. But then I learned that you weren't questioning me…"

I interrupted, "I wasn't questioning you. I would never question you. I just wanted to know things. I wanted to know why…" I trailed off.

With kindness and patience she continued, "I realized you weren't questioning me, you were just asking questions. It's how you understand things. But I had to learn that about you."

I stared at her, blinking. I'd never had anyone explain me to me before. Not like this, anyway.

Sitting across from my principal in that moment, this striking realization came over me. I'd almost immediately realized that every time my teaching partner would suggest a new activity, a change in our delivery model, or new program idea, I'd replied with what I now realize was a response that made her feel as though I was questioning her – her knowledge, her expertise, her experience. I would offer

51

suggestions for how to take a learning experience to what I thought was the next level instead of welcoming her ideas. What my partner heard was me telling her that her ideas weren't good enough. What I heard was that I wasn't a team player. There was a massive communication breakdown. We had failed at communicating on every level both personally and professionally. And rather than fixing it, because we were both feeling unheard and hurt, we worked as two silos in one room. Neither of us were ready to try; we'd already decided the other wouldn't be willing. How could we expect our students to collaborate when we couldn't even model it ourselves?

To fail, at its base level, means to be unsuccessful. I was not successful in making my teaching partner feel heard, appreciated, or respected. I had failed. That was one of the most difficult years of my career. The tension that existed between us was thick. You could feel it as soon as you walked into the room. We weren't happy. The anxiety was high. On most days, school was the last place I wanted to be. Our relationship was beyond repair and I didn't know how to rebuild it. I write today from a different lens than I lived that year. It would be easy to list the, "Yeah but, she [insert examples of things that were said and done]." but where does that get us in the end?

Don't get me wrong, we need to acknowledge our feelings, our hurt. We need to give ourselves time to process these less than ideal situations we find ourselves in. We need to be able to regulate ourselves when our emotions are high – something I was trying to teach my students and was having an extremely difficult time doing myself. We need to give ourselves grace, time to feel our feelings. We also have to be able to sit back and look at the situation from someone else's perspective and take time to understand how to change our own behavior.

When we practice empathy over apathy, situations that have us drowning suddenly become clearer. And if we can't do that, at the very least, we have to be willing to listen to why or how we failed. It's not easy. It's not fun. It's hard to hear. The word *fail* in education is an ugly word. It's an unpleasant thought to sit with. It carries a terribly negative connotation. But until we're willing to really hear it, to sit with the discomfort that comes with it, we're never really moving forward.

We need to experience failure. And we need to reflect on that failure. When we reflect on failure it becomes less about what didn't work and more about how to make it work moving forward. When we reflect on failure it becomes less about how we screwed up and more about how to do something better next time. When we reflect on failure, we grow. And isn't that our number one goal? To be a better version of ourselves tomorrow than we were yesterday?

I attended Springfield College in Springfield, MA, USA as an undergrad from 1989–1993 and loved my time there. Springfield College made me the person I am today. Since graduating in 1993, not a week goes by that I don't think of something that makes me smile or a lesson (good or bad) I learned from my time there. I've stayed connected to the school over the years and even have a Springfield College Humanics philosophy triangle tattooed on my leg, "Spirit, Mind, Body." So to say I have a fondness for my alma mater is an understatement. So in 2016, when I graduated from Boston College with my Ed.D (I also have an eagle tattoo because I loved my time there, too) I was honored to be asked to be on the Springfield College Alumni Council.

It was a six year seat and I was so excited to start. For my first meeting, I walked in with my Springfield College shirt and a smile from ear-to-ear. The alumni council members were asked to set and share their individual goals for the year. The few council members before me said:

"This year, I will…"

- Recruit a new student to visit Springfield College.
- Donate to the Alumni Fund.

- Wear my T-shirt to my son's high school events to promote the college.
- Volunteer at homecoming.

And then it came to me…

"Welcome to the council, Matt. All those goals sound great for a first-year member. What do you want to set as your goal this year?"

"I want to be the Springfield College commencement speaker once during my term," I shared.

Silence came over the room. Then I heard a few giggles and saw people looking around, unsure of how to react.

At the time of the meeting (September 2016), I had just finished my tenth year as a principal and completed my doctorate a few months earlier. In September 2016, I had not yet published an article, written a book, or spoken outside of Massachusetts. But that was my goal, so why not put it out there?

The council chair looked at me smiling and did not know how to ask me a follow-up question. So I looked to my left and waited for the next person to share. Finally, the chair said, "Matt, that seems very lofty for any member or even a trustee."

"Thank you," I answered.

A few members came up to me at lunch and asked if I was serious, and a few others who knew me said, "Dude, that was a funny way to announce your presence on the committee."

However, for the following reasons, that really was my goal over the next six years:

- I loved my school.
- I wanted to speak at the graduation because I believed (and still do) I had things that would inspire new graduates.

- I wanted to push myself, not just wear a shirt or attend quarterly meetings.

My goal never changed. Every year at the September meeting, when it was my turn, I shared my one goal: "I want to be the Springfield College commencement speaker once during my term." But May of 2022 came and went, and I was never asked to be the commencement speaker.

Did I fail? Was I a failure as a committee member? After that first meeting in September of 2016, during the ride home, I reflected on my goal because of the stunned looks on people's faces. I asked myself, "What do I need to do to reach my goal?" My answer was to do something impactful in the field so I could earn the honor of speaking. So I began trying to do just that.

I started by collaborating with Tech and Learning Leader in October 2017 as part of my new role as a District Director of Digital Learning. Over the next few months, I drafted six articles on different topics I had for their publication. In February, I was informed that one of my submissions was selected. I was so excited. My work was going to be in a nationally published magazine!

When I shared this excitement with some educators in my district, including my superintendent, their responses were, "But five were not. That's less than a 20% success rate." Why do we focus on failure in this profession? I knew my superintendent's negativity was because of his jealousy and lack of drive, but his attitude was a buzzkill.

Others I told also focused on the fact that five articles were not accepted. I guess people were just used to a culture constantly focusing on the negative. My focus, however, was on the one article that got accepted. I viewed the process as a success. A month later, there was a magazine with my work and my name in it. Scan the QR code to check it out.

55

Over the next four months, I was asked to write more pieces for Tech and Learning Leader magazine, attend a few out-of-state events, and even speak at some of them. Again, I followed the same logic and turned in five to six drafts each time, often only having one accepted. Every time one got picked for publication, I felt proud and did not focus on the ones that did not go to print. In fact, for the topics that did not get accepted, I repurposed the ideas in some other way.

September 2017 came, and it was time for my second Alumni Council meeting; I was ready to share my goal. This time I had magazines with my work in it to show the chair. More work samples. Do I ever learn? Once again, it was soft giggles and awkward looks but even more so because I shared I was published. Each year I went back and shared my same goal; however, I never brought any more evidence of my work. And to be honest, that was sad for me.

I never did speak at graduation. However, when I completed my six years of service, I had been an annual guest speaker in a Springfield College education class and had published over 40 national articles in Tech and Learning, District Administrator, ASCD, and Edutopia. I had the opportunity to be a featured speaker at several events and published three books. So, did I fail because I did not reach my goal? During the last meeting some Alumni Council members even pointed out that I never reached my goal.

Why do we focus on shortcomings and negativity in our field? Part of my motivation for writing this book is to encourage others to focus on their successes and accomplishments. It's okay to be proud of your work and achievements. Disrupting the status quo is not about doing random things differently to be a rebel; it is about shifting the norm when it is not enhancing the common good. There is no way I would classify my six years on the council as a failure because I didn't reach my ultimate goal. The number of educators I supported, many of whom I never met, helped me reach the true goal I reflected on while driving home after that first meeting: what I had to do to be worthy of being the commencement speaker.

Failure is a topic educators rarely want to discuss. This is because we always look at it as "I am a failure" as opposed to "That didn't work, what did I learn from it?" or "How do I make it work next time?" We don't often know how to deal with failures because we have not built our inner confidence. We are a profession that focuses on the negativity that surrounds us. Evaluations always focus on what we didn't do and what to do next time. When the state assessment results are posted, we go right to who didn't pass. Stop. Seriously stop perseverating on what didn't work. If we are going to disrupt the status quo, let's build our confidence and keep trying and celebrating attempts.

The successes I have enjoyed the most in my career often followed a failure or missed attempt. Look back at the story of my first published article. Five submissions were turned down, but the sixth submission was printed, and I was so proud.

So, where do we begin to build our confidence? Successful people have used visualization in their work, sport, or craft for ages. This is not new, except in education. We plan for "when it goes wrong" all the time. We have back up lessons or other ways to give us an "out" if what we plan doesn't work. Flip that! Think about what you want to accomplish as a teacher, and visualize yourself achieving those goals. I was thinking about standing in the Springfield Civic Center delivering a speech for six years and used that to drive me. Visualizing yourself successful will give you self-assurance and make you feel ready and confident to reach your goals.

The bottom line is that imagining yourself as more confident will make you more confident! We hear, "I will believe it when I see it" all the time. Change that. *If* you believe, you *will* to see it.

So how do we start to believe it? I love Nike, but I don't always believe "Just do it" gets it done, especially if you don't know where to start. I can't say, "Just be more confident." That's not how it works. So here are a few strategies to build your confidence, push you out of your comfort zone and into the learning zone, and set goals that make people giggle.

Whenever I've learned something new, I've rarely gotten it on the first try, and if I did, it definitely wasn't perfect. Priding yourself on being a learner will allow you to remove unrealistic expectations of yourself, be vulnerable, and take risks in your learning.

When insecurity creeps in, and it will, try to stand tall. I have learned that body language speaks volumes. For example, when you are not confident or feel like you're going to fail, you tense up, walk with your head down, and look around to see who is looking at you. Standing confidently and owning the moment, even when you don't feel it, will increase your confidence and positively impact your chances for success. I always ask, "What is your walk-up song?" Meaning, if you were walking into the boxing ring or up to plate in baseball, what song would you want to play to get you pumped up? Have that song play in your head when you are standing tall.

At all costs, I try to avoid negative people. Yes, there are negative people in schools. So the work of creating a positive community is ongoing. Recognizing that there are toxic people in your building is a start. Once you do that, ensure you are not surrounding yourself with them. Although all educators face challenges, it doesn't help to constantly focus on them. Being around negative people limits your confidence in trying something new because you worry about what people will say if you fail. Negative people will always point to your failures when you mention trying something outside the status quo. They will continue pushing you to stay in your lane and play it safe.

One struggle I have as a leader is recognizing my strengths. But I know I have them, and so do you. How do I know this? I see talented teachers doubt themselves all the time. Even teachers who need improvement have strengths, but we don't point them out. While it might be uncomfortable at first, recognizing your strengths does help to overcome negative self-perceptions. Celebrating your strengths will ultimately lead to confidence.

I understand facing failure is not easy and by no means am I suggesting that. I know the first time you confront failure, you might feel hurt, disappointed, or mad, but that's alright. It's human nature, and we've all been there. Just don't stay there. Doing things outside your comfort zone or trying new things will help you prepare mentally for future failures and allow you to celebrate attempts.

Any profession is a roller coaster ride. There are moments of success and satisfaction, and times of failure and dismay. However, we must change the perspective of failure because we would be less capable of high achievement without it. Failure is the key to success. Attempts are where growth and satisfaction are born.

I am anxious. I'm anxious in the morning. I'm anxious during the day. I'm anxious at night. The dark, quiet, silence of an empty bedroom at 2 a.m. is a breeding ground for the anxious thoughts of a person like me.

My anxiety didn't just come out of nowhere one day. It didn't hit me when I became an adult and suddenly had the responsibility of a career, a house, and the lives of two helpless infants; although if it had, no one would have blamed me. My anxiety has existed since the day I was born. A predisposition nurtured by an intense and traumatic childhood resulted in full-fledged, clinical anxiety and depression.

While I wasn't diagnosed with anxiety and depression until my twenties, my anxiety presented itself years before that. There was the fear of leaving home. The fear of driving alone. The fear of using a public restroom. The fear of initiating a conversation. But regardless of the specifics, the biggest fear I had, the fear that fueled every anxious thought, symptom, or tendency, was the fear of failure.

In high school, I put scrap paper in between every single page of my notebooks. Why? Because I couldn't write in pen; I was too afraid of making a mistake. So, instead, I wrote in pencil. And pencil, when you write on the back of a page, smudges onto the previous page. I couldn't have my notes smudge, and I couldn't cross out with a pen, so my anxiety devised a ludicrous system of doubling the size of every one of my notebooks to prevent smudging, yet still allowing me the power to erase.

Failure for someone with anxiety is like an arachnophobe facing a spider. It's terrifying; debilitating. But even for someone without clinical anxiety, failure is uncomfortable; scary. I'm not an arachnophobe, but I hate spiders. I have no interest in talking about them, looking at pictures of them, or being in the presence of them. But the difference between spiders and failure is that exposure to spiders doesn't serve me any major benefit. Exposure to failure, however, does.

Failure is not only necessary, it's inescapable. No matter how hard you try, the day will come when you fail at something: making the tying shot in the last second of a high school basketball game, maintaining a friendship or relationship with someone you once loved, getting a job you want. Failure is omnipresent. It doesn't exclude anyone. How thoughtful, right?

So while I was terrified of failure, I had no choice but to come to grips with it. I had to find coping skills to deal with the prospect of it, and strategies to deal with the presence of it.

We've all heard those famous examples of failure: Michael Jordan being cut from his high school basketball team. Oprah Winfrey being told she was "unfit for television news" and subsequently released from her first job as a tv anchor. But we all have stories of failure. Babies don't just stand up one day and successfully walk down the hallway with the stride of an adult. Young children don't typically hop on a bicycle, no training wheels, and ride down the street unassisted.

Nearly every task we've completed in our non-academic lives is one at which we likely failed in our first attempt, and probably miserably. Walking, talking, using a utensil, skating, writing out a check; nearly every task. But outside of academia not successfully completing something the first time is not only completely acceptable, it's expected. So why do we change these expectations the minute the classroom doors close and the task becomes multiplication, or thesis writing, or showing how environmental conditions impact the rate of enzymatic reactions? What is it about school that makes us think we should know how to do something after seeing it done once?

"Alright, Johnny. Today I'm gonna show you how to ride a bike."

"Okay, Uncle Fred."

Johnny is standing next to his uncle holding his first bike; no training wheels. Up until this point, Johnny has only ever ridden his Big Wheel in the driveway.

"Now watch how I hold the handle bars and throw my right leg over the bike." Fred demonstrates as Johnny watches.

"I put my foot on the pedal, get it lined up just right so that I can push forward and start moving with enough momentum that I can pick my left leg up, get it onto its pedal, and sit back on the seat. Ready?"

"Yeah," says Johnny.

"Here we go!" yells Fred and off he rides.

After swinging the bike back around, Fred yells to Johnny, "Okay, bud! Your turn!"

Without any assistance, Fred is not holding the bike to help Johnny balance, Johnny throws his right leg over the bike, aligns the pedal, pushes forward, and…

We know how this is going to end. Johnny is going to push off, tip the bike to one side and hopefully get his foot down in time to catch himself. In the real world, Johnny would try again, ideally with Fred's direct assistance. But in the classroom, if we modeled this lesson after the way in which we approach all failure, Johnny tips the bike, Fred lets him know he wasn't successful, and they move on to something else.

If the standard is that all kids learn how to ride a bicycle, and the goal is to meet the standard, why would Fred give up when Johnny failed? He wouldn't, at least not forever. Perhaps they work on it for an hour that first day, and Johnny still can't ride the bike. Maybe the next day they take a break from bike riding and try something different. But

Fred fully intends on revisiting the bike riding because again, the goal is to meet the standard and the standard is to ride the bike. Yet in academia, this is the exact opposite of how we approach learning.

And then there is the greatest irony of all of this too: sure, Johnny failed to ride the bike, but didn't Fred fail too? Fred didn't meet his goal either: getting Johnny to ride the bike. But in the world of academia, we are so quick to label the students as having failed, but we can't dare say the teachers did, too.

Many school districts where I work are designing "Portraits of a Graduate" that include "whole child" statements. Sure, we want to educate the "whole child," but only after they can memorize the unit circle, describe the three branches of government, and write a five paragraph essay. So let me ask you this: when you think about your schooling experience and its influence on the skills you apply in your daily adult life, does it directly correlate? I bet most of you said, "Nope."

When I was a classroom teacher, I used to make fun of the unit circle. I would tell my students, "You can't tell me why you chose a specific scientific procedure in your lab, but I bet you can tell me the cosine of $2\pi/3$."

"Negative $1/2$!" they would yell back in unison.

"See," I told them.

I was a science geek in high school and a mathlete. Yup, I was on the math team. My senior year, I took 35 periods a week; seven classes a day. Of those 35 periods a week, 13 of them were math. A little more than one out of every three classes I took my senior year was a math course. And today, not only do I not use a single thing I learned in those math classes, I couldn't even tell you what the cosine of $2\pi/3$ is; I had to look it up.

What I do use on a daily basis, however, are my communication skills, the ability to explain what I'm feeling and thinking, flexibility, coping skills to deal with the unexpected, and a willingness to try something different knowing full well it may not result in the desired outcome. If Fred sticks with Johnny and doesn't "grade" him on his first attempt, not only will Johnny meet the standard, and Fred his goal, they will both have worked on their communication skills, their ability to explain what they're feeling and thinking, their flexibility, their coping skills to deal with the unexpected, and a willingness to try something different knowing full well it may not result in the desired outcome. This is the whole child. And this, we know, happens regularly outside of the classroom. So how do we bring it into the classroom?

First, we have to completely change our mindset around assessments. The goal should never be to "get it right." Instead the goal should always be to learn something new, and I'm not talking about how to ride a bike, or what the cosine of $2\pi/3$ is. I'm talking about YOU! Learn something new about yourself, your thinking, and how to solve a problem, not answer it.

Once we change our mindset around assessments, we can begin to design tasks for students that support our philosophy. Every product you ask students to submit should be an extrapolation of their thinking and show that. No matter what the specific standards are, they can all be boiled down to the same thing: clear communication of a thought process. And it's this growth in thinking that should constitute a grade.

While I loved science in school, I hated labs. They were nothing more than an exercise in following instructions and getting a prescribed answer. You got an A if you got the answer, and a C or worse, if you didn't. In college, as a biology major, I remember meeting with my academic advisor and asking her how many more lab sciences I had to take because I hated them so much. Her response? "If you don't like labs, I suggest you change your major."

Because I have the biggest chip on my shoulder and am driven by trying to prove people wrong, I remained a biology major and became a teacher. I vowed that as a teacher, I would make the lab experience better for my students. It would be about inquisition, trial, error, and curiosity. So I did just that.

Labs were never a single day or class period in my course. Rather, labs took place over multiple days. They were all designed the same way. I would present students with a question: How do environmental conditions affect the reaction rate of the enzyme catalase? From there I would set up and show my students how to run a control, i.e., a general lab procedure with defined amounts of reactants. Once all students could successfully set-up, run, and collect adequate data for the control, it was off to the races. They were asked to document the things they wondered while setting up the lab and the questions they had about the outcome. From there, students were told to satiate their curiosity and try to find an answer to one or more of those questions. Students started manipulating variables and re-running experiments. There was more data, more questions, and even more trials and errors. Sometimes we would be in the lab working off one control for three days.

The students took still images and videos of their experimental trials. They collected data, organized it, and analyzed it visually. The conclusions they wrote included deep reflection about their original questions, their procedures, their analyses and even further questions they had, and additional experiments to run. Students organized their "lab reports" in the form of structured presentations. Because every group was asking different questions, every lab was different. Watching each group present what they wondered about and what they did in the lab, was engaging and thought provoking. Their grades were never based on whether or not they successfully figured out the right correlation between enzyme rate and optimum conditions. Instead it was based on how they communicated their thinking. And if they couldn't get their experiments to run properly by the end of our time in the lab, that was okay too. They simply needed to discuss what they did, what they think went wrong and why, and what they would do differently the next time.

In my science class, the students' entire lab experience was falling off their bikes, getting back on, and trying again, a.k.a. failure. Because my focus was on the process, and the rubrics I devised were all the same (same components, same expectations, and same point scales) by the end of the year, they sounded like expert scientists no matter where their data led them. This, I told them, was real learning. Failure, I explained, was a necessary step in all scientific discovery, as it is in all the most important discoveries they were yet to find out about themselves. The most essential lessons we learn in life come from legitimate problem-solving, I told them, not problem answers. Because what has more longevity in the world of the average person, the cosine of $2\pi/3$, or the experience of learning a lesson of your own creation?

Scan the QR Code to find some of the lab activities I designed and completed with my students.

1100 1011

Since as far as I can remember, calling parents about their child was typically done as a means to change the behavior of the student or report something that has gone wrong. I did this. A lot. It would get to the point where I knew certain parents were tired of hearing from me, and quite frankly, I was tired of calling them time and time again. Nothing seemed to change. Until I changed.

I started calling parents to tell them what their kids were doing well, rather than always what they we doing wrong. What I noticed almost immediately was that my entire classroom dynamic changed for the better. Parents were happy to hear from me and I was excited to call home. Students even began to ask when their parents would hear from me as they knew they were crushing it at school and were hoping to go home to happy parents.

This narrative shift didn't begin with the telephone, it began with me re-evaluating the notion of assessment in my classroom and that began with redefining what it meant to fail at school. In the context of failure, we often hear students asking what they got as a numerical value out of 100. With a freedom to fail, students began asking me,

"Can I try this?" instead of, "What did I get?" This idea was one that was instilled in me after an early school year meeting with a group of parents. As I sat in the meeting, a parent asked me, "Why do you focus on his weaknesses at school when he will pursue his strengths in life?" This changed everything. My feedback. My assessment. My evaluations. Everything.

Up until now, feedback seemed to be about making corrections. It meant fixing what was wrong rather than expanding on what was right. Much of this thinking stemmed from my beliefs about classroom management. In my experience, quiet classrooms were the best managed. Or so I thought. I used to think the volume of the classroom dictated the quality of the teacher. I now know learning can be loud and can be messy. Loud classrooms aren't necessarily managed poorly and quiet ones don't always indicate learning is happening. In reality, the discussions should be accountable talk. But in many ways, I would punish loud groups and assume they were off task.

I did the same with homework. Those who would "play" school always got stickers because their homework was always finished on time. In fact, these students typically had their homework done before they even left school. I used to keep kids in at recess for not completing homework. I now realize they didn't do the homework, not because they didn't want to, but because they didn't know how to and had no one to ask. The problem with homework is that it often highlights inequalities.

This was a large paradigm shift. I had been in school myself for 25 years, both as a student, and then as an educator. Incomplete homework meant detention. Not only was I punishing them, but I was punishing myself, too. I also needed a break!

You'll notice a pattern to my writing. "I used to think…and now I think." These moments of reflection are crucial for growth, and speaking matter of factly, our students cannot adopt this kind of thinking in graded contexts because grades imply failure is wrong and mistakes are bad. What I came to learn was that kids don't hate learning. They hate the intimidation of timed testing environments and the embarrassment of being labeled wrong. I ruled my compliant classroom with intimidation. My class may have been quiet, but my classroom management sucked.

I improved my teaching when I focused more on creativity and collaboration and less on compliance. Instead of trying to catch kids doing things wrong, I celebrated the amazing things they did well, and those *things* got exponentially better because the fear was gone.

When I shifted my thinking from *delivering* curriculum to *discovering* curriculum everything changed. Kids began to explore, inquire, be creative, think critically, and collaborate. Recognizing curriculum in these authentic contexts provided the best teachable moments I have ever experienced.

Much of what I have reflected on came from a shift. I began my teaching career understanding that middle school teachers "run a tight ship." My colleagues congratulated me for making my students sit still. And quiet. So very quiet. I was proud. I was really proud. Classroom management was *the* number one skill to have, I was told.

But it wasn't working.

I was tired of yelling. I was tired of scolding the same kids, day in and day out, for the same behavior. It took me a long time to let this go. If there was ever a power struggle, it had to lean in my favor. Until it didn't. And what a sigh of relief that was.

I was popping less Tylenol. I had fewer headaches and my voice box thanked me for the break. I started asking students about their interests and their passions. I took a genuine interest in them – both, my students and their passions. I began designing my curriculum based on their explorations and less on my teacher's guide and textbooks. When I removed the textbook from the equation, I was forced to also remove the quantitative tests and quizzes it also gifted us with. Don't get me wrong, the textbook can be a great resource, but it should never be the only resource, especially in the era of connection.

I had a clean slate.

I had no agenda other than to meet students where they were and help them move forward.

I realized that my students' mental health was way more important than any test score. Ironically, and unintentionally, this approach not only made us all feel better, but our standardized test scores also improved. The less we taught to the test, the better the test results got.

We were creating independent thinkers. Problem solvers. Collaborators. And most importantly, content creators.

Some of the best passion projects were created that year. I will never forget an eighth grade student building a six foot tall Arduino-powered candy dispenser. It even took real quarters! There were a plethora of curriculum connections to this project, and I was getting cavities from the Skittles!

Another big project that year was done by a group of three boys who dismantled a lawn mower motor. After convincing administration that it was okay to take apart a gas powered machine in Mr. A's eighth grade class, we got down to business.

I knew these boys came from families of mechanics and greasy projects was where their interests were.

"What size lawn mower is that?" I asked.

"It has a 24 inch deck," one student replied.

"Oh?" I asked.

We were studying circles in our measurement unit of math. It had never dawned on me that the length of a lawn mower blade when compared to the circumference of the lawn mower deck is, quite simply, 3.14 units smaller, or pi. Up until this point, I would fill student workloads with packets of activities. I expected students to find the circumference of race tracks and other circles on paper that were typically meaningless to any context a 13 year old would understand.

When it clicked that the circumference of a lawn mower deck is equivalent to the length of the blade multiplied by pi, everything changed. I was certain these students would never forget this. I know I haven't.

But this project didn't end with math. It also didn't begin with math.

It began with trust.

I trusted my students to work alone, outside, on this motor.

I trusted my students to stay on task while truly exploring their passions.

The curriculum came second.

I'll never forget this same group of students showing me the lawn mower oil cap. It had a sticker on it that read, "5W30." Not only were we studying circles in math class, we were exploring particle theory and viscosity in science class.

My mind was blown.

"What is the difference between 5W30 and 10W30 motor oil?" I asked.

They told me it was about thickness.

"We call that viscosity," I said. "Just like how some ketchup pours faster than others."

I love telling this story because this group of students was the same group I would holler at for not finishing their packets of work in a timely manner. But now? Now they were making truly authentic curriculum connections to their own world.

And this isn't even my favorite part of this story.

I will never forget walking outside to check on this group as they were tinkering away. During this class time I would conference with different student groups as I engaged in their learning. I would travel from group to group, showcasing what other groups were doing and how it related to our curriculum. It became a gallery walk.

As I approached my future race car mechanics, I noticed a man beside them wearing dirty overalls. Concerned, I approached the man and asked why he was here and if he had checked into the office.

"Mr. A, this is my uncle. He owns the shop uptown. We called him to help us. You always say to find the experts. We found ours."

My. Jaw. Dropped.

I had created an environment where my students used the resources available to them to solve the problem. They called the expert mechanic uncle. And he came straight from work.

In a previous classroom, I would have lost my mind if a student jumped on their phone without permission. But in this case, it was celebrated. I was so proud of this group. I was proud of every group, but this one was special. Our relationship had taken a 360 degree turn for the better. So did our mental health, and so did their test scores. I truly believe this is directly correlated to the new level of confidence they found in themselves. School was no longer about test scores, grades, or failure. It became a place for them to shine, for them to showcase, and for them to share their skills with the rest of the class. It became a place where they were leaders.

PERSPECTIVE

I was walking down the hall towards my first and second split grade classroom like I do every afternoon when the recess bell rings. But this time I heard a colleague call my name.

"McMenemy!" she shouted. "I didn't even have to look at their faces and I knew they were your kids!"

I stopped and cringed. I could feel my shoulders tense and my jaw clench. The only thought that went through my mind was, *Oh God, what did they do now?* A handful of my students had a bit of a recess reputation. It wasn't uncommon to get a visit after the bell from a colleague or administrator. I'd watch one or two of my students make every attempt at avoiding eye contact only to immediately throw one another under the proverbial bus. Half the time they would get pulled out and spoken to, the other half I would smile, nod, and say, "I'll talk to them." all the while thinking, *what's the big deal?*

I turned around to see my colleague holding two tree branches in the shape of a Y. I knew what I was looking at. Unbeknownst to me, my students found the branches at an earlier recess, gathered supplies from the classroom later in the day, brought everything back outside, and…built slingshots.

I shook my head but couldn't hide my feelings. She could read my body language.

I stifled a laugh and smiled at her as she said, "I knew you'd be proud."

I started laughing. I couldn't help myself. Thankfully, she did, too, as she said something along the lines of, "Only your kids would have the know-how and imagination to build these." I often wonder why this is the case. Is it me? My routine? Is it that I encourage them to explore and try new things? It's not the first time I've heard something like this. I've always chosen to take it as a compliment. This time it actually was.

While my first thought was mild concern for my students' impending targets, my second thought was immense pride. So much of what I do in our classroom focuses on building innovative, outside the box thinkers who creatively problem solve and persevere through the challenges I throw at them. They were five and six years old. By June, they'd exceeded every expectation I had.

I had automatically assumed their impending targets were not their fellow humans or small woodland creatures that ventured into the school yard. When we step back and look at the bigger picture, these kids meant no harm. In fact, they were exploring math in nature using their own creative instincts to build tools.

So as I stared at my colleague holding the slingshots and shrapnel from their recess escapades, I couldn't help but think about the creativity and planning that went into building these new toys…or weapons…tomayto, tomahto. All kidding aside, this was a teachable moment; an opportunity to assess. Where I live, we evaluate skills like collaboration and initiative. These kids were certainly collaborative, engaging in authentic math play that I had nothing to do with it. If that's not initiative, I don't know what is.

In sharing this story of innovation and creative engineering with others, half of my audience stared, shaking their heads. But I knew it was not because they were in agreement with me. I had become accustomed to their perspectives after 20 years in the classroom.

As I saw it, my students hadn't built tools for destruction or violence. They hadn't sat with malice and planned a recess battle while they snacked on apple slices and animal crackers. They had done exactly what I had been drilling in them since the first day of school. A piece of cardboard is never just a piece of cardboard. An elastic band is never just an elastic band. And a tree branch in the shape of a letter Y is never just a tree branch in the shape of a letter Y.

Perspective. It's always about perspective.

Our perspective, the way in which we view things, our attitudes towards people and circumstances, will always shape the outcome of any situation. Assuming the worst would have made for a very different after recess conversation. When recess ended and my slingshot engineers came down the hall, they immediately made eye contact with me and the color drained from their faces.

"Did you build slingshots outside?"

Nod.

"Did you build slingshots to hit people with?"

Head shake.

"When you build slingshots, most people think you're going to use them to hurt people. Did you know that?"

Head shake.

"Can we save building slingshots for when I'm around, so we can build them together and choose safe targets?"

Nod.

"Are you hungry?"

Nod.

"Go eat your snacks."

They looked at each other, smiled, and scurried away.

At only six years old, they automatically assumed they didn't have a side of the story to share. They immediately thought they were "going to get in trouble." Why is that? Has school become a place of blame and guilt? Are we using fear to gain compliance? These kids had been in school for three years; most of the first two occurring from behind a computer screen while learning remotely from home. How had they built this definition of school so quickly?

When my co-authors and I sat down to brainstorm a list of ideas and topics for this book, I pitched a section called, *What's the big deal?* As I tried to explain my rationale with not enough coffee in my system for our early morning meeting, all I could articulate was the idea that when I listen to educators complain about students' behavior, more often than not I'm thinking, *What's the big deal?*

We settled on Perspective.

Now, admittedly, my students' creations were confiscated before they had the opportunity to inflict damage on anyone or anything, but I believed them. Those two had never given me any reason not to. When we trust our kids, we empower them to make choices they can be proud of. With trust comes respect. With respect comes autonomy and love. And this is the true definition of classroom management. It is not based on fear. It is based on love.

My students saw the entire experience from an *"ooh, what does this do?"* lens which was why I was so proud. For every time they've asked, "Mrs. McMenemy, what happens when…?" I've answered, "I don't know. Why don't we find out?" And as far as I was concerned, that's exactly what they did.

In the last week of August, colleagues sit with class lists, rearranging desks, making name tags, getting everything ready for back to school. It's customary for others to look at the lists of names and give unsolicited opinions of students. These conversations are always a part of the new school year I try to stay away from; I want to be able to form my own opinion of my students.

One year, as I rearranged furniture, unstacked chairs, and sharpened pencils, a colleague walked into my classroom. The sole purpose of her visit was to warn me about a student.

"I saw your list," she informed me.

"Uh huh." I knew where this was going.

"You have So and So. His brother is So and So."

I was fairly new to the school. I didn't know many students by name. I did know the older brother, by reputation only – one that preceded him.

"Okay," I replied.

She read the confusion on my face, "He's THAT kid."

Part of me wanted to shut her down and give her a hundred and one reasons why I disagreed with her line of thinking, but most of me just wanted her to leave. So I smiled, thanked her for the heads up, and continued sharpening pencils.

Turns out that year was the year I had a class full of *Those Kids*. It was *That Class*. I was given a very special group of kids who would require every ounce of energy to figure out exactly how to tap into what they had to offer. They were all so incredibly different, and yet all looking for the same thing – someone to ignore their labels and come to understand and accept them for who they were and where they were, not where they were supposed to be. Our job is to teach the kids we have, not the ones we wish we had.

I've always loved *That Kid*. Every version of *That Kid*. The kids who can't sit still. The ones who ask too many questions. The ones who require every ounce of patience you were graced with. These are the kids that make us better, but only if we choose to see them that way. These are the kids who force us to look inward. Your perspective on who they are and what they have to offer will always define the kind of year you're going to have. It's no different than deciding you're going to have a bad day before your day has barely begun. You know those mornings when you wake up feeling unrested? Your neck is sore from sleeping wrong? You stub your toe on the way out of your bedroom only to discover you're out of coffee? Those days when it's just one thing after the other and before you've even left the house, you've already decided you're going to have a bad day? We all have those days. When we focus on the labels our students are given, when we choose to view them through a lens that focuses on how they're going to make our classroom life difficult, we're never giving them a chance to prove us wrong. When our perspective changes, so does our day. When our perspective changes, so does our classroom. When our perspective changes, the opportunities for growth increase exponentially.

For better or worse, our perspective changes everything.

I have been called a "leader" since I was hired as an elementary school principal in 2006. The issue with me being called a leader was that I knew nothing about being a principal besides some classes I took as part of my certification program. I had never held a position as a school leader, and to be honest, I'm not sure I was the best choice. I learned later that I was hired because of my connection with Apple and because I was young and impressionable. The new superintendent used me like a minion to carry out some of her otherwise unpopular ideas.

So, I had my name and the title of "Principal" on my office door, a nice new business card, and a special parking spot in the faculty lot. A parking spot? Yes, a parking spot, which I quickly got rid of. I felt like it created a separation between me and the staff, plus I'm not that special. I found it more valuable to rotate the spot, give it to an expecting mother, or someone with an injury. As for me, I was a 34 year old, somewhat fit guy who could walk a few extra spots to work if I needed.

So just like that, I was a leader. The day before I got the offer, I was a District Educational Technology Professional Development Specialist, and the day I accepted the job, I was a school leader. Anyone who met me on the first day of my principalship already looked at me like a leader for no other reason than the title I had. That realization always bothered me and still does. I walked into that school in 2006 without experience, yet I had clout because of a title. Sadly over the next 16 years, I would see individuals who held positions of leadership referred to as leaders just because of those titles. But were they really leaders? Not all of them!

We have all worked for a boss we didn't like, was rude, or even under-qualified. Yet each one of them was still considered a leader because of their title. This thinking has to shift. Being in a leadership role does not automatically make you a leader.

Leadership can be discovered in any role in our schools, from the custodian to the parent volunteer, to the teaching assistant, to the teacher leaders, and most importantly, the students! We have to change our perception of what or who a leader is. We must keep the perspective that leadership is what individuals do, not who they are.

Looking back on my career, I can tell you I was not a leader in my first year as a principal. I was a taskmaster and more like a lifeguard than a leader. Every day I was just trying to ensure people didn't sink. That didn't make me a leader; that made me a guy with a business card that said "Principal" who ran around putting out fires. It took years of experience, failures, and mentorship to possess the leadership qualities that matched my title. Half of the authors of this book have never held a school leadership position, yet they are global leaders in the field of education. I will say it again: leadership qualities and actions are more important than a title.

Additionally, popularity and likability do not automatically grant an individual the title of leader. Neither does being the loudest, the snack provider, or the most veteran. I learned this early in my leadership journey. When I was a junior in college, I was Vice President of the Class of 1993. However, it was not because of my leadership skills but because more people knew my name when it came time to vote. I know that now and if I am honest, I knew it then too.

In addition to my role as vice president, I was also a new student orientation leader, a popular student, well-liked by staff, and friendly with many different social groups. People would joke and call me "Joe Campus."

Because of my popularity, I saw myself as capable of anything. If you asked most students, they would say I was a student leader because I was outgoing and would do shots with anyone at the bar. But I wasn't a leader. I had untapped potential, but I didn't want to look in the mirror, admit my shortcomings, and grow into a leader. I just wanted to hear from others that I was a leader.

The most powerful leadership lesson I learned occured in March of 1992. I've shared in every one of my books, including this one, my admiration for Springfield College and how well they prepared students to possess leadership qualities after graduation. Well, this one lesson wasn't taught to me in any class or program; it was delivered to me by sophomore Marc Cicciarella.

Leadership Training Conference (LTC) is a program at Springfield College for campus student leaders. They take the student leaders of clubs and student government off campus for a three day leadership retreat. Additionally, LTC has six student LTC leaders who are specifically selected to lead a group of students at the retreat. LTC weekend also hires outside professional speakers to lead activities and teach leadership lessons.

I attended LTC in the fall of my sophomore and junior years because I was the Class of '93 Vice President. After winter break in January of 1992 and attending LTC as a junior, it was time to select the six student leaders who would guide the groups at next year's conference. I actually remember thinking to myself, *Do I even need to apply? Of course, I'm going to be one of the six.*

I went through the motions, filled out the application, and had my interview with the student chair for next year's event. I went into the interview very cocky; I was going to be a senior, and I was "Joe Campus." I perceived myself as a shoo-in. But that is not how the story goes.

A week later, I went to the post office to get my mail (in 1992 there was no email). I opened P.O. Box 426, pulled out a letter, and began reading:

"Thank you for your interest in the role of LTC student leader. I regret to inform you that you are not one of the successful candidates. Thank you for all you do for Springfield College."

Sadly my first thought was, *Did I get the wrong letter? This can't be; I'm Matt Joseph, of course, I'm going to be one of the LTC leaders.* I was even ballsy enough to go to the chairperson's room, he was a resident assistant in my dorm, and ask him if I got the wrong letter. He looked right at me and said, "No, you didn't." I actually think he was happy to say that to the cocky kid who thought he was a shoo-in.

I threw the letter out and quickly did what so many "leaders" do when they feel wronged, I started making excuses and cutting down the process. We need to look at ourselves in situations like this and think, *How can I grow from this experience?*

I lived on the fourth floor of Alumni Hall with my friends. A great way to lose perspective is by surrounding yourself with friends who tell you what you want to hear. When I told them I didn't get LTC student leader, they all said, "Dude, you should have gotten that role." We see this all the time with "leaders." They surround themselves with "yes" people and cheerleaders who tell them they're great. A true friend, however, would support them in tough times and share areas of improvement for them to work on.

Enter Marc Cicciarella, a student who also lived on the fourth floor of Alumni Hall and attended LTC that fall. He was a sophomore, shorter than me, and popular within a small circle of friends. In my cocky opinion, Marc was not as popular as me, and not someone I looked to as a leader. I saw Marc more like the kid down the hall who might join us if he wanted to feel "cool." I was an arrogant fool. He was not really a friend, but a good guy, and I had no issue with him until that day. But let me just clarify at the onset, I know now that my issue had nothing to do with Marc. My issue had to do with myself; I just had the wrong perspective. What happened next was one of my biggest regrets as a student and as a leader, but it was also one of the most significant moments of growth I never knew I needed.

Marc came down the hallway smiling because he saw me outside my room. He had a letter in his hand, an LTC letter to be exact. I knew at that moment he must have applied, but I knew there was no chance he got selected. I mean, *I* didn't get selected. How could *he?*

To my surprise, Marc said very excitedly, "I got selected. I'm so excited to be one of the student leaders with you at LTC." Again, his perception, because of the way I carried myself and my status at the school, was that I would get selected.

When Marc told me he got picked, what do you think I did? Just like anyone who has to eat humble pie, I was a jerk. I said, "There's no way you got it, and I didn't." At this point, some of my friends came out into the hallway. I asked them, of course, to make myself feel better, "Can you believe Marc got in and I didn't?" All my friends said the same thing, "No way!"

I'm sick even typing this now because of the person Marc is. He's a genuinely selfless person and someone I look up to. Marc never admitted to how much I hurt him or talked about it because he is a class act, even to this day. I was beyond selfish.

My behavior also fractured any kind of friendship Marc and I had. Instead of using the moment to improve myself, I turned my back on LTC because I thought they wronged me. I then surrounded myself with more "yes" people to tell me how "great" I was as my senior year approached.

November of my senior year rolled around, and as much as I wanted to put LTC out of my head, I couldn't. I knew that in order to prepare for LTC, the leaders and participants had three meetings in October to get to know each other and the structure of the retreat. I had yet to face the fact that I didn't earn the position of Student Leader; I still thought I was robbed. I even went so far as to say they were jealous and didn't want me to outshine any of the six group leaders. But, again, I was wrong.

The Wednesday before the trip was supposed to leave, I got a knock on my door. It was Marc. We had rebuilt some of our friendship because he lived two townhouses down, and my townhouse, Townhouse 15, always had the best parties, some of which Marc attended. I was a little shocked to see him, but said, "What's up, Marc?"

He asked if he could talk to me; I was a little confused. I actually thought he was going to address the fact that I was awful to him the previous year. But he didn't because he's someone with true character. Instead, Marc looked me in the face and said, "Someone dropped out of my LTC group, and I need a creative, outgoing student who has already attended the pre-meetings. The first person I thought of was you. I want you to join my team because it will be a valuable weekend, and you would bring a lot for the others."

I was blown away. Of course, I wanted to go! I loved doing all the collaborative activities on campus, but I would never admit that because I didn't get picked to be a leader. I looked across the table at this kid who was a year younger than me, who I was incredibly rude to and embarrassed a few months earlier, and I was speechless. For people who know me, that doesn't happen too often. Sadly, my first thought was also one from the wrong perception: "Are you messing with me?" I asked him.

Once I realized he wasn't, I swallowed my pride. This kid had the courage to walk over to a townhouse of eight seniors and ask me to be part of his team. The amount of leadership he showed in doing so is something I will never forget. It was the slap in the face I needed to go from the cocky college kid who didn't earn the status I walked around with, to the humble beginnings of the leader I always hoped I could be. I quickly realized at that moment that your actions and your character earn respect, and that is what makes someone a leader. Marc Cicciarella is a leader.

Of course, I went to LTC, which was an unbelievable experience. I left the "Joe Campus" aura behind and went away with an open mind. The lessons I learned from the social interactions that were not my "yes" people, and the training content I received was top notch learning I still use today. I cannot thank Marc enough for his courage and leadership in showing me what a true leader does. He knew my skills and what his team needed and put his feelings aside to do what was best for the team. Even knowing I would be energetic and outgoing and possibly draw unwanted attention to the group, Marc found a way to lead the group and highlight each member's skill.

I actually stayed at Springfield College for one more semester to complete my student teaching in the fall of 1993, and guess who was the student chair of next year's LTC event? Yup, it was Marc, and again, he asked me to join his team, this time leading my own group. I never tapped into my own potential until I gained the correct perspective of Marc's qualities and leadership skills. Because of Marc's mentoring and guidance I came to learn what true leadership was.

Marc and I preparing for the 1993 LTC event. Him as the leader, me as the learner.

Leadership is not a title. Leadership is not having a staff of "yes" people. Leadership is not a false bravado. Leadership is about your actions. Leadership is about never forgetting anyone, because anyone, I mean, anyone, can be a leader regardless of what is printed on their door or business card.

Fitness is important to me. Between running and working out, on average, I exercise three to five times a week. I do this because I like the way it makes me feel and because, for me, managing my anxiety and depression is a multitiered approach. Yes, I am medicated. Yes, I see a therapist weekly. But I also exercise regularly, take my diet very seriously, go to bed and wake up at the same time every day (including weekends), and drink a lot of water; a whole lot of water. In fact, I drink so much water, I became tired of carrying around multiple bottles of water, having to refill my cup, glass, or reusable bottle, and finding myself thirsty without any water around. So, in 2019, I decided to simplify my life. I started carrying around a gallon jug of water no matter where I went: to work, to every meeting during the day, grocery shopping, to hockey games and practices, to family functions, to the zoo, to sit on the couch. You name the place, if I was going, my gallon of water came with me.

Of course, my new companion was curious to many. I got inquisitive looks, odd glances, and a lot of comments and questions:

"That's a big bottle of water." Yup.

"Do you take that everywhere you go?" Yup.

"Do you drink all that water?" Yup.

"If I drank that much water, I'd be running to the bathroom all the time." Yup.

Walking around with a gallon of water solicited the unedited remarks of people still searching for their adult filters. It rivaled the days of being pregnant or just postpartum and being told I was adorable, huge, swollen, looking uncomfortable, and in need of wearing a belly band. It was a free pass for everyone else to tell me exactly what was on their minds. *Why*, I thought to myself, *couldn't people just have a better perspective?* There was another human being growing inside of me; stealing my own nutrients to the point of nausea, causing me to hold fluids to the point of neuropathy, and moving around to the point of insomnia. I'm sure you would look phenomenal if you felt sick to your stomach, numbness in your hands and feet, and sleep deprived all day.

Perhaps this is an extreme example, but it does get the point across. In regards to my water jug, if I walked into work with a jug of coffee, I guarantee the comments would sound more like:

"I feel ya."

"I love coffee."

"I need that much coffee in the morning, too."

"Where can I get a jug of coffee that big?"

Water, the very thing that sustains life, that allows your body to perform all the necessary functions for survival, is seen as a crazy thing to be carrying around. But coffee, *that's* relatable. The one thing we have in common with every other person on this planet, staying alive, is considered the anomaly, but something we *might* have in common is normal. Consider this perspective for a moment. What sense does it make? It would be like questioning someone for breathing air during the day, but high-fiving them for smoking pot.

Perspective is a crippling hurdle in education. Because we take perspectives that are most common to our own experiences, we pigeonhole ourselves into only being able to relate to a given population of students. In its deepest iteration, perspective simmers as implicit bias. In its most simple form, perspective is an unfavorable classroom rule.

There are so many perspectives for just about anything you can think of: a political topic, a rule, a confusing statement, a diet, a call in a game, a stand-up routine. Perspectives are what fuel conversations and debates, connection and dissension, growth and learning. The simple fact that there are endless opinions in the world makes life intriguing and curious. If there was only one perspective on any given topic, what purpose would it serve to talk about it?

Education should welcome perspectives; encourage them, in fact. Teachers should never make decisions until they've considered at least one perspective other than their own. Learning doesn't occur unless you are exposed to concepts and ideas that are novel to you. But too often, people are married to being right; it's the kryptonite for learning.

U.S. politics have become a topic of conversation I refuse to engage in unless it's with a select few people in my inner circle. There are very few people I have met who can sustain a friendship with someone who has a different political perspective than them. U.S. politics have destroyed relationships in my life. Participants in such conversations cannot, or will not, see any other perspective than their own. They can't fathom that people might think, feel, or interpret things differently. Their perspective, their way of thinking, is the right way of thinking, and everyone else, whether their mother, father, sister, brother, uncles, or seamstress, can go to hell.

Being right is why things are banned from educational institutions. It's why politics are a no-no in the K-12 classroom. So why are people so beholden to being right? Why are so many people willing to lose relationships over it? Because being right is nothing more than a need to be in control; to have power. It happens in the classroom all the time. Take the following situation for example:

Mrs. Miller's fourth grade class is putting away their social studies lesson and preparing for a math activity. As the students return to their desks and begin looking for their math sheets and pencils, Mrs. Miller asks the class for their full attention once they are ready.

"When you've found your math sheets and you have your pencils," Mrs. Miller continues, "please stop talking and look up at me."

As the students shuffle through materials and find the necessary items, Mrs. Miller waits patiently at the front of the room. She reminds the students of the expectations once they are ready: "Heads up, ready to actively listen when you're ready."

The final students settle in and Mrs. Miller begins the lesson. "Please make sure your name is at the top right hand corner of your math sheet," she requests.

Unfortunately, as one student is writing his name on his paper, his pencil snaps. "Shoot!" he says in an exasperated whisper.

"Shhhhh," hushes his groupmate.

"Sorry," he apologies.

While Mrs. Miller is asking for a volunteer to read the activity objective at the top of the sheet, the student is wrestling through his desk for another pencil; he can't find one.

"Students will be able to..." another student goes on reading the objective while he tries to solve his pencil problem.

He nudges his groupmate to get her attention. "Do you have another pencil I could borrow?"

"Huh?" she states, having been focused on her classmate reading out loud.

"Can I borrow a..."

Mrs. Miller yells his name. "I told the class, 'No talking!'"

"I was just..."

"To the office, please."

"But I was just..."

"To the office, NOW, please!" repeats Mrs. Miller.

He puts his broken pencil down and stands up at his desk. Slowly he makes his way to the classroom door feeling the eyes of all his classmates on him. Mrs. Miller has already continued on with the lesson. "Thank you. Now who can..."

We've witnessed, or heard, similar situations in the classroom many times before. The only reason the student is headed to the office is because his teacher failed to have a perspective other than her own. Mrs. Miller perceives the situation as him being defiant and not following expectations. He, however, perceives it as Mrs. Miller being unfair because he was simply asking for a pencil so he could actively listen and participate.

As a school administrator, I deal with situations like this all the time: "The teacher sent me to the office because I took my phone out. But there was no time left in class and we were all lined up at the doorway anyway."

"The teacher asked me if I wanted to take a seat, and at the time I didn't, because I was still working on the group project. So I said, 'No, I'm still working,' and he kicked me out."

"I got a zero on the assignment because I passed it in a day late. I understand that I shouldn't get full credit, but I did it, and I got all the answers right. I can't even get partial credit?"

There is no right or wrong answer to any of these scenarios, yet some approach each of them as if there is not only a right answer, and it's their answer. We talk about teaching the whole child. We talk about providing students with lessons that are greater than the curriculum in which we teach. What are these situations teaching our children? They're teaching our children that being right is more important than being fair. That the only life-long learners in the classroom are the students themselves. And that in every situation, there is only one perspective that matters, that of the person in charge.

I wrote a co-taught elective for high school seniors back in 2010. The course was a science/history elective called Science and Public Policy. The entire course was centered around one question, one theme: just because we can, should we? Students engaged in science lessons (viruses, bacteria, cell division, alternative resources, warfare technology) and history content (conflict, politics, law, policy, government). But the course standards were all skills-based. Students heard multiple perspectives on all the controversial topics we discussed and had to formulate an argument of their own, either written or oral, with supporting evidence. The goal was never to prove someone wrong. Rather the goal was to listen, consider all the facts, and state a single perspective. It wasn't about being the loudest, or angriest. It wasn't about being right or wrong. Students were graded based on how thoughtful and insightful their perspectives were; how actively they listened to others' opinions. Perspective, we taught them, was a conversation, not an argument.

Every single one of the examples provided above could have been solved if the teachers forced themselves to consider one other perspective before coming to a conclusion:

"Is everything okay back there? I see you are talking to your neighbor who is trying to pay attention. Is there something I can help you with? Do you need a pencil?"

The teacher who sent the student to the office for his cell phone could have realized that her allowing students to line up at the doorway in anticipation of the bell ringing communicated to kids that class was over. If class was over, then surely it was okay to look at your phone quickly; what would you be interrupting?

The teacher who sent the student to the office for not taking his seat could have considered that his student was still productively engaging with his classmate at the time in which made his request. The student answered his question. Had the teacher said, "Please take your seat," maybe the student would have. Instead, the teacher seemed to leave it up to the student to decide.

Teachers are inconvenienced when students pass in papers a day late. But are students being graded on the course content, or their timeliness? The student even indicated she would be willing to accept partial credit. Simply meeting the student halfway, saying "I acknowledge your perspective," would have made the student feel heard and kept the relationship positive.

Perspective is the root of nearly 100% of the conflict we face. The jobs of educators are hard enough already, why make them harder? If we simply asked questions before jumping to conclusions, nearly all teacher-student conflicts could be avoided, and maybe we could get back to the real reason we're in the classroom: to learn crucial things like why drinking a gallon of water a day is so goddamn important.

1100 1011

My world drastically changed on the evening of Friday, March 13, 2020. In fact, the entire world changed that night. International borders were being closed across the globe. I was in Grand Rapids, Michigan where I was the scheduled keynote speaker at the Michigan

Association of Computer Users in Learning state conference. That keynote never happened.

"You better get back to Canada! They are shutting down the borders."

I remember arriving home and looking at my wife. We didn't say anything, but we knew we were in trouble.

I had resigned from my school district as an eighth grade teacher in 2017 after spending twelve years in the classroom. My computer science consulting had taken off and I was poached by a local university to join the Faculty of Education. It was the perfect opportunity. The perfect dream job. Three sections of online teaching to adult learners, and a chance to expose as many young students to computer science as possible.

That Friday the 13th was much different than usual. Typically my wife and I celebrate with an 80's themed tribute to Camp Crystal Lake. We didn't say much that evening. We watched the news and stared at the lake. In the blink of an eye I had lost all consulting and speaking opportunities for the foreseeable future. My three university sections were not enough for us to make ends meet. Fortunately my wife was still teaching, but it was only half time.

Unlike most Saturdays, the next morning felt eerily quiet. No one was outside. No cars were passing by. No smiles for miles. I remember noticing my neighbor walking across our lawn. I thought that was a bit strange considering the context. Maybe he was just checking in on us?

Knock knock knock.

As I opened the door I noticed him smile. He looked different than usual. He was wearing a boot for a sprained ankle.

"We need to talk," he said.

This can't be good. This neighbor was known on the street as the one to keep happy. I was about to find out why.

"Your free range chickens are coming onto our property. We are going to be planting soon. This cannot happen."

"Of course!" I agreed.

The chickens never went on their side, he just assumed they did. The chickens were never allowed to wander unless we were outside. It was the wild rabbits that were eating his gardens.

"Good, because I called the town," he stated.

"You did what?"

"I called the township. You cannot have birds."

"That isn't true, we've done our research."

I tried to reassure him the birds were fine and that we were allowed to have them. I thought I had him convinced but he was looking for a fight. I remember thinking this lockdown had us all quite emotional.

I was standing in my kitchen on the first day of lockdown being chewed out by my neighbor over hostas he hadn't planted yet. The first day I was officially unemployed. He had no idea what was in my head, nor I in his.

Over the next several weeks we continued to let the supervised chickens wander. It was all we could do. It was a reason to be outside. I remember seeing his family point out the window from their own side as we could only hang out with those we lived with.

Our relationship with them had always been positive. Their son was in teacher's college and I tried to help as often as I could. He even did a placement in my wife's school and she drove him there daily.

But lockdown. Lockdown messed with all of our heads.

I remember sitting outside, having lost count of how long we'd been at home, watching the birds and wondering why they were so curious.

Aren't we born curious learners too? Does school ruin that for us? I still laugh watching the chickens roam like a primary school soccer team chasing the ball. They move as one unit.

"Keep your (expletive) chickens on your side!" I heard my neighbor scream.

Lockdown messed with my head.

I hollered back, "They are, mind your own business!"

And with that, we had a shouting match from one property to the other because Heaven forbid we break a lockdown rule and cross property lines.

"I came to your house that day out of respect for you! I used to like you!"

Just like that, we were speaking in past tense.

"Well, intentionality over impact!" I yelled back. "You don't get to come into my house and blast me with everything you think we do wrong around here the day I lost all work gigs for the foreseeable future."

There was no way I was self-regulating. I was stressed. I was anxious. I felt helpless.

Lockdown messed with my head.

Many things come to mind as I reflect on this experience. For starters, some people focus on the now, not what came prior. The work we did attempting to get his son a teaching job meant nothing compared to the hosta garden. And that is okay if that is what they choose. But learning is a process. End of unit tests and exams focus on the now, not where students have come from. We need to celebrate the process. We only learn to walk by falling down. But most importantly, he was not able to see past his intentions. In his mind, he intended to show respect. But his actions were perceived as bullying and threatening.

93

I like to think back to my intentions as a first year educator. I intended to have great classroom management skills but that was perceived as yelling. I intended to bedazzle my students with engaging lessons but that was perceived as burnout by my colleagues. I intended to focus on student voice but wouldn't listen to a word they had to say. It was my classroom and while my intentions were good, the impact was devastating. I ruled with an iron fist and made compliance my only means to an end. I remember colleagues celebrating me for keeping them quiet and I wore that like a badge of honor. As a result of this style, we never did group work. Students never collaborated unless they were marking each other's spelling tests.

I've learned a lot since that first year. Most importantly, it is okay to be where you are. It is not okay to stay there. Afterall, we got into this business as lifelong learners.

It wasn't until a few years later that an eighth grade student's parents really got me thinking about perspective. In my first year, *my* perspective was all that mattered.

Once I had a few years of teaching under my belt, I moved up to an eighth grade classroom from fifth grade. This was my happy place and certainly where I found my niche. I have many people to thank for this and two are definitely worth mentioning.

My administrator that year decided he was going to *see* school through a student lens.

"They are always on their phones. And that is okay. Maybe I will try it too."

So for the first few weeks of school, his office remained closed and locked and his computer remained powered down.

"This is the world they live in. I want to be invited in," he would say.

"We need to stop trying to make kids conform to our world, but instead, embrace theirs." I replied.

That was the year a student's parents changed my entire perspective. Their son was in my class. His brother, just one year older, was in my class the previous year. They were practically twins, just a year apart. Both boys were autistic. The older son was working on a modified program as per the expectations outlined in his IEP (Individualized Education Plan). I do love that term. I think we all need IEPs because we are all different. Imagine that!

The older son had moved on to high school and mom and dad were not too happy about the transition. He went from a school of 300 kids to a high school of 1000 kids with little support. They were afraid the system would eat him up and he would become another data point. Essentially this ninth grade student was working at a third grade level the year prior and now the expectation was he would be in ninth grade with support as needed.

It didn't surprise me that the parents requested a meeting with me about the younger son. He was working at grade level according to the tests he was given in elementary school. But because he looked and acted just like his older brother, he wasn't challenged much.

On meeting day, I rushed down to the office at dismissal. I already knew the parents well and was looking forward to another school year with them. The resource teacher was also present. From left to right was me, my principal, this student's parents, and the resource teacher on my right. We sat in a circle at the table so we could all see each other. I noticed mom was already crying.

Uh oh, I thought. *What the heck happened?*

"Okay, thank you all for coming," my principal began.

"May I start?" Dad asked.

As he stood up I noticed him reach for his right jean pocket. In it he had a wad of paper. He slowly unfolded it and took a very deep breath.

"I have a dream," he began, pulling from the infamous Martin Luther King Jr. speech.

"I have a dream that my child will be a functional member of society. I have a dream that he will hold down a job, make a good living, and have conversations with people like we are right here. But until you change something about his school system, I'm afraid that will never happen. Please, I'm begging you," and he now wipes away tears, "I am begging you to change his school system. He has autism. He punched people to get out of French class because he doesn't like French class. Please stop suspending him and understand his perspective. His report cards are filled with Cs and Ds but he has a million pieces of Lego at home and I can grab one at random and ask him which kit it belongs to and he is right every single time. Please, in his last year of elementary school, with a progressive administrator and a techy homeroom teacher, please do something to make my child feel successful."

I'm tearing up now as I write this. This story, almost a decade old, still feels fresh. It feels fresh because it is fresh. It's fresh because it is still relevant.

As the meeting wrapped up and the Kleenex box made its third trip around the room, we all agreed to just stop the school system he was accustomed to. I was so eager and excited to try new things with everyone's permission. I was stoked to explore the possibilities and unlock the potential this kid had because when dad said *Lego*, I heard *Minecraft*.

Fortunately our students had iPads, so purchasing the pocket edition of Minecraft was a no brainer.

The very next day, I bought him Minecraft.

"Have you seen this?" I asked.

He shook his head no.

"Why don't you go and try it and come back in a few minutes."

He nodded and lit up because anything was better than the worksheets someone was scribing for him in that moment.

I was eager to see how well he could use this as a tool for learning. But what came next was something I never thought possible. He had built our classroom in Minecraft. He had his own desk. He was showing me what he sees. He was showing me how he sees our classroom. He was giving me a much needed perspective. *His* perspective. And it was quite different than mine.

I remember receiving an email from his mom in the coming weeks asking when our school book fair was. On the arrival of the book fair, Mom showed up at the beginning of the day.

"Mr. Aspinall, he has never gone to the book fair before. I've never seen him read a book. He wants three books. He wants three Minecraft books."

Just like that his math and literacy programs were reborn. When you consider a Minecraft block as a unit, say one cubic meter, that world becomes Mathland. Minecraft became a space with few rules where this student could build growing patterns. He built different representations of swimming pools to show volume. He built castles and mazes so we could explore probability outcomes of getting out alive. He was reading books and he was presenting his world to our class. For the first time, we saw the world how he did.

Finally, we had some perspective.

His French teacher and I collaborated with a French math task and he started going to French class. He built aquariums and geographic regions. He built country flags during the Olympics and told me about sports data. I saw the curriculum in everything he was doing and it didn't require a single textbook, worksheet, or better yet, a scribe. I never want to just *cover* the curriculum. I want students to *uncover* the curriculum. I want students to *discover* the curriculum!

We put Minecraft in his IEP. That legally made it his tool for learning and all of his educators needed to embrace it. It is not about us, we need to stop trying to make kids conform to our world, but instead, embrace theirs. Minecraft was his portfolio of learning and it changed everything for him. And us.

VOICE

In our first grade classroom one year, we had two class pets: Sheila and Sammy the goldfish. The kids named them, fed them, watched them, and took care of them. Every single day. Sheila and Sammy happily swam in their tank that sat right atop the counter next to the jars of pencils, markers, and crayons.

One morning we noticed Sheila swimming a little more sideways than upright. After a Google search and a trip to the pet store, we treated the water in the tank, waited, and hoped for the best. Not a day or two later, what I knew would happen, happened. I walked into the classroom to find Sheila floating upside down. In an effort to avoid five and six year olds being traumatized, I scooped her out into a little plastic cup. It was decided Sheila needed a burial, so we took her in her little plastic cup, outside, past the school yard, said a few words, and buried her next to a tree.

As the morning continued the students shared their feelings, made connections to their own lives, and asked questions I tried to answer as best as I could. By day's end, our little goldfish and her funeral were fleeting thoughts in an otherwise hectic day in a first grade classroom, or so I thought.

Over the next few days, our lives in the classroom continued as normal. One thing stood out, however. One of my students was a little more emotional than usual. We had our ebbs and flows of classroom behaviors, as all classes do, and his behavior wasn't atypical. But he was a little more impulsive than usual; quicker to get angry and it was taking longer to help calm him down.

Over the course of the year, I had built enough of a relationship with him that I was usually able to pinpoint the cause of his escalated behaviour. This connection with him allowed me to be more proactive with him rather than reactive. It was exhausting, but it was necessary for his benefit, and mine; except this time. Behavior is a form of communication. I knew he was communicating, I just couldn't decipher what. No matter how many conversations he and I had, no matter how many times I asked for the reasons for his choices, he wouldn't tell me. I would later learn it wasn't that he wouldn't, it was that he couldn't.

I had his mom on speed dial. We had a very open line of communication and our only goals were his success and happiness in the classroom. Our definitions of success, while very aligned, changed based on how he started his day. After multiple phone calls, and scratching our heads, we were unable to figure out just what was going on in his little head. We started making small talk. She was also a teacher and our days had a lot in common. At some point in our conversation, the topic of our goldfish came up. I assumed she knew about little Sheila in her plastic cup, left beside the giant tree just passed the school yard. It was a big classroom event. She asked me when it happened. There was a pause. The pause told me everything I needed to know.

I would come to learn that he had a brother and his own very personal experience with death and loss. Everything seemed a little clearer now. We don't always use our words to communicate. My little friend had made a strong, difficult connection to his own world and it was affecting him deeply. What he needed was someone willing to listen; for his voice to be heard. When I moved schools three years later, he handed me a letter he'd written. One single line written by a nine year old would forever remind me that no content we teach will ever outweigh the importance of listening to our students; of having their voices heard. *"You always listen to my side when everyone thinks I'm doing something wrong."*

The first thing we need to do to create learning environments where students have a voice is to listen. I was listening, by observation, and knew something wasn't right. In my early years I would have been impatient with such behavior. I wouldn't have taken the time to really consider what was going on or even known to consider that there was more to it than what was being presented on the surface. When our students are given a voice, our classroom changes. Fostering student voice meant I had to let go of the notion that, as an educator, I was solely in charge of what happened in our classroom.

Over time and with experience, *my* classroom became *our* classroom. What I've come to learn is that our students won't necessarily ask for, or tell us, what they need with their words. They won't always clearly communicate their thinking; it will almost always come through their actions. Listening, whether through observation or otherwise, allows us to make decisions that make our classrooms one where our students are respected, valued, and treated with dignity. Sometimes we'll make really amazing decisions that turn our classroom into incredible learning spaces, and sometimes we'll stumble across them accidentally.

One year, I bought a pencil sharpener for the classroom. I spent a fortune on it (as far as electric pencil sharpeners are concerned) and proudly displayed it on the shelf at the front of the room but not before my A-type personality decorated it with a "TEACHER USE ONLY" label. It was perfectly centered on the sharpener so no one could miss it. It was shiny and had nice bold capital letters, and it would quickly become the bane of my existence.

I'd sit down to work with students and hear, "Mrs. McMenemy! Can you sharpen my pencil?"

I'd be at the back of the room and, "Mrs. McMenemy! Can you sharpen my pencil?"

I'd walk into the hallway and they'd follow me out with, you guessed it, "Mrs. McMenemy! Can you sharpen my pencil?"

There were days I'd walk in at the 8:15 bell and, "Mrs. McMenemy! Can you sharpen my pencil?"

But how?! You literally just got here!

They never needed their pencils sharpened when I was standing beside it. And every time I suggested they grab a sharpened pencil from the jar, somehow there were never any there. Sharpened pencils seemed to exist in the same universe as the socks that go missing from the washing machines.

So, I did what I had to do. I let the rarely seen B-type personality take charge and rip off the A-type's ridiculous label. The A-type cringed, but B-type knew this was the only option. This would be the first domino to fall in what would be a year filled with more student voice than I ever imagined.

It took weeks to undo the damage that label did in the three days it survived on that pencil sharpener.

When I would hear, "Mrs. McMenemy! Can I sharpen my pencil?" I would reply, "You can. This isn't my classroom. It's ours."

I began to respond the same way every single time they asked for anything. So much so, that there came a point where their classmates would reply on my behalf. We finally got to a point where anything they could reach in the room was fair game for all.

I used to be of the mindset that doing things like this would be giving up control and be the beginning of the end. I behaved as though it would put me on some slippery slope that would start with them sharpening their own pencils and end with a pig's head on a stick in the middle of the classroom. What I would eventually come to learn was that I wasn't giving up control, I was sharing it. And in the end, I realized it was never about control, it was about mutual respect.

Our classroom became a place where students didn't ask to do things anymore, they told me what they were doing, er...politely let me know. Well...not always politely, but we quickly curbed that. This wasn't an easy task; for them, or me. School is a place where we have to ask permission to have our basic needs met. "I'm thirsty. Can I get a drink?" "I have to pee. Can I go to the bathroom?" "I'm hungry. Can I eat my snack?" The way I see it, learning in any classroom should also be considered a basic need and not something you should have to ask for. If you need a ruler, you should be able to get a ruler. If you need to sit on the rocking chair to read, you should be able to sit on the rocking chair to read. If you need a device to research a piece of information, you should be able to get a device (and probably a charger) to research the information. If you need a break, you should be able to take a break. At the very least, my goal was to teach my students to understand their needs so they could have them met. They were six and seven years old. They needed me for so much, and then one day, they didn't. And isn't that our job? Give them all the tools and strategies they need to fly, and then watch them leave the nest and soar? And boy, did they soar.

I often worried that running a classroom like this would result in the whole give an inch, take a mile adage. And sometimes it did, but never for very long. When that label came off that pencil sharpener, I'm pretty sure 30 kids lined up to use it, and I only had 20 in my class! Were they purposely breaking pencil tips, just so they could sharpen them? Yup, they were. Did they sharpen the erasers off the back to see what would happen? They most certainly did. Were they breaking pencils in half and sharpening both sides? You betcha. Did this happen with almost every new inch I gave them as the year unfolded? Without a doubt. Did it make me want to pull my hair out? A-type had no hair left but B-type knew this wouldn't last. B-type told A-type to be patient and wait. B-type was right.

I didn't have the idyllic class of angelic students who colored within the lines. No, no. I had a class of 20 five and six year olds turning six and seven who spanned the spectrum of learners from their own life experiences, their understanding of themselves and what school was, and their ability to self-regulate on any given day. Not only did we color outside the lines, I taught them to draw the lines themselves. I was watching first hand how listening to students – what they say, what they do, what they don't say, what they don't do – and then making decisions with them, not for them, was the key to a learning environment where every student could be met where they were and grow at their own pace.

I was once the educator who would hear about the things going on in a classroom like mine and just assume it was complete chaos. And if you stood at the door of our classroom, that's maybe what it looks like, chaos. But (on most days) you'd never be more wrong. Empowering students to be leaders of their own learning and advocates for their own needs and the needs of others is loud and usually messy. Though, not the kind of loud that drowns out the voices of the quiet. In fact, quite the opposite. The kind of loud that makes sure every voice is heard – whether that voice is a classmate or a teacher, heard through words or seen through actions. As for the messy part? It was never a mess we couldn't clean up, literally or figuratively.

The key was that our classroom was built on mutual respect where having their voices heard was as much an expectation on me as my voice being heard was on them. What I hadn't realized would happen was how much we would lean on empathy and compassion to exist in a learning environment like this. Their voices being valued meant they were invested in everything that happened in our little community. They were empowered. When our voices are heard we feel connected on a deeper level to a bigger cause. When our voices are heard we are involved in the process of growing towards common goals. When our voices are heard we become a much bigger part of the equation for success – no matter how we choose to define what that success is.

And the most beautiful part of all this, is that I learned it from them.

When I started to reflect on the topic of voice, the first thing that came to mind was that a school leader's voice is just one of many. Too often, principals feel their voice is more important or more impactful than others. But I see the principal's role being the following:

1. To create a safe environment for staff and students.
2. To create the best learning opportunities.
3. To make every staff member better because of their leadership.

To make the third goal possible, I advise school leaders to "Get out of the way." Yes, you read that correctly: "Get out of the way." Over my 17 years in school and district leadership, I have seen many teachers fail to reach their full potential because of the micromanagement of their building principals. I went through a phase early in my time as a principal where I thought I was the most important voice in the building. I could play the boss card, and my name was at the top of the chain of command.

But it wasn't until I started listening more and talking less that the schools I was tasked to lead made strides. When I say "Get out of the way," I don't mean go to the local coffee shop and spend the day watching Hulu. What I mean is, set the vision and direction you want for the school, then ask questions about how to achieve that vision. Don't give directives and expect they will just get done. Teachers have the closest proximity to the students. Their voice comes with practical day-to-day experience. Combining their voice with the leader's experience and big-picture vision, will allow a school to excel. Leadership is not a one-way street.

I was an elementary school principal when I was writing my dissertation. My biggest goal for the school year was to incorporate peer observations into our school. My studies at Boston College gave me the foundation to share with our educators that this practice positively impacts student learning. However, I should've stopped at sharing my vision with the educators and then let the educators have more say. But as most of the stories in this book have gone, I did not do that. Instead, I went into the meeting with volunteer educators who wanted to support launching this initiative and told them how it would roll out. I was well organized, and made check lists of look-fors, scheduled dates, times, and who would visit each classroom. Educators, as you read this, I'm sure you're cringing at how upper management this sounds, because you're right! I thought I was being organized and supportive, but what I was doing was micromanaging (well, controlling) the staff. I cut out all the educator voices yet they would be the ones carrying out the initiative.

The educators in the room quickly said, "That's not how this will go." Thankfully it was my fourth year as principal, and I had built a culture that allowed teachers to speak freely. I am glad they did because what was to follow became the best initiative in my ten years as a principal. One of the teachers said, "Can we have the last 55 minutes of this meeting just for us?"

My inside voice said, "Hell no, this is my idea, and I will tell you how it will go." But my outside voice said, "Sure. Come up with a plan that works for you, keeping the vision at the core. Then we can meet to review." I walked out of the meeting thinking, "Well, there goes my idea. This isn't going to happen." 55 minutes later however, I was asked to come back into the room.

They shared they wanted to move the initiative forward, but with the following:

- They changed the initiative's name from peer observations to classroom visits because teachers don't do observations.
- They created a digital sign-up sheet for interested educators.
- They wanted me to budget for substitutes to allow teachers time to visit classrooms.
- They created expectations for the visiting educators and the teachers they were visiting so it was a mutual learning opportunity.
- They wanted me to cancel the next two staff meetings and use that time to let teachers start visiting classrooms without students in an effort to eliminate discomfort with the idea.

We spent the next two days planning the classroom visits and making the initiative a reality.

At the next staff meeting, the teachers who came up with the specifics explained the process. Again, the principal does not need to be the voice that shares everything. The most powerful part of the process was having the teachers share the initiative and show their support for it.

Following the explanation, we broke up into groups with one grade level representative in each. The teachers spent ten minutes in each one of their groupmates' classrooms allowing the teacher to explain their space so they would understand what they were walking into during visits.

Over the next five months, we went from seven teachers visiting classrooms to 14. The goal for the next year was to have every interested staff member participate. The initiative became part of the school culture and how teachers learned. It was the most powerful professional learning we could've had, and it all happened because I got out of the way. What the educators needed the most from me was not my voice but my support. And they got it.

Providing teachers a voice means you energetically seek their intake and feedback. Intentionally invite teachers to participate in decision-making that directly impacts them. In addition, encourage educators to be part of discussions like interviews or enrichment programs. They should have an active role in providing feedback that will be used to make important final decisions.

When principals give teachers a voice, the teachers feel valued. Feeling valued was the number one finding from my doctoral research on improving teacher job satisfaction. In my opinion, the fastest way to value educators is to give them a voice. Doing this will help educators feel empowered and develop a sense of ownership. With ownership comes buy-in; a direct line to teachers supporting school-wide initiatives. As educators feel more included, they'll develop a sense of collaboration and will be more likely to advocate for your decisions. So how do you get there? Creating an open, emotionally safe environment where teachers have a voice takes time.

One of my co-authors, Christine, loves the musical Hamilton. In one song, Aaron Burr sings, "Talk less, smile more." When I started as a principal and sadly even as I gathered experience, I would over-talk and often dominate meetings. Someone close to me said, "Stop that!" Her comment snapped me out of my talking marathon and made me realize I needed to let educators do more of the talking. I realized I had to create an environment that let educators express their ideas, ask questions, share answers, and solve problems.

When you need to talk, say, "Can I ask a question for clarification?" or "May I make a suggestion." Trust me; you'll be positively surprised by the reaction you get. Remember to always thank people for their contributions. You want to show and express your openness for what they are offering. "Talk less, smile more."

It has been incredibly important for me to make sure to communicate from the start of any initiatives when educators will be directly involved in making final recommendations. It is also important to communicate when you will make the final decision and how you will use their input. Being transparent will help build trust. Gathering information is the first step; following through is the next one. Your credibility diminishes the first time you don't follow the teacher recommendations you ask for. Educators will see that your actions don't match your words and will be reluctant to participate when you request for their input a second time.

I understand that you can't always follow teachers' suggestions. When this is the case, tell educators why! Be as transparent as possible when talking to an individual, a committee, a team, or the entire faculty. Then, after ensuring them of your commitment to follow through on their suggestions and concerns, explain why you can't at this time. In this field, you might encounter unforeseen barriers such as comments from the District Office, current policies, district procedures you weren't aware of, privacy, etc. Being transparent shows you respect their voice, even if you can't use it.

I know it's more timely to make decisions and take action based on what you think and want. It takes a lot more time and effort to seek others' input and allow them time to reflect, make suggestions, and give feedback. But the long-term benefits of giving teachers a voice is invaluable. Allowing educators to be heard leads to empowerment, teacher leadership, improved morale, and partnerships. You will still be responsible for multiple daily decisions as a school leader. But when you can, involve those who impact students the most. No matter how long it takes, it's about getting it right for kids.

I have always been more driven to ensure the success of an initiative when I've had ownership over it. I had to take this approach when talking to teachers about their classrooms. I had to give them control of the learning space. Allowing teachers to create their own layouts and bring in their own furniture, lights, and plants allowed them to take ownership. Their classrooms are where they spend the majority of their days; let them use it as they see fit. If a teacher sees value in taking their class outside, allow it! Students deserve a mixture of learning settings customized by innovative teachers. And teachers deserve to work in a space where they feel comfortable.

When I go to education conferences, I like the ability to choose the sessions I go to based on my needs and interests. I've always wondered why we don't do this in schools. Why don't we offer educators differentiated or personalized professional learning opportunities? Voice and choice in professional development is essential for educator growth. I don't believe in forcing teachers into professional development groups based on subject areas or grade levels. I understand sometimes this may be necessary, but why not rotate groups according to purpose or interest? Let educators pick the paths that focus on areas they feel they need or are interested in. As a result, engagement will increase, and individuals will improve in areas where they are weakest.

Given my experience, I can confidently say that educators, not the curriculum, are a school's most essential resource. Unfortunately, district policies often squash teacher talent because of constraints. Free teachers from a scripted scope and sequence. For instance, allow teachers to experiment with project-based learning or maker spaces. Support teachers who are taking risks and failing forward. Your leadership vision has to include a consistent message that encourages creative experimentation. Educators are reenergized when they are allowed to try new things!

Nothing in these examples requires considerable effort from administration. What it does require however, is listening, a mindset of support, and a lot of saying yes to teacher ideas. If you do this, your building will become a place where people want to work and where students want to learn. Everyone grows when we treat educators as the leaders they are and ensure their voices are heard.

TW: Mentions of sexual assault.

There were many sayings I heard growing up:

It could be worse.
You'll be all better before you're married.
It's my way or the highway.
Be careful what you wish for.
Shit or get off the pot.
It takes one to know one.

Rarely did any of the sayings I heard as a kid upset me, or leave me wondering about their impact on my life years later. But one in particular affected me deeply; left me intimidated, quiet, and quite frankly, terrified.

Kids, I was told, should be seen and not heard.

At the time, I just thought it was some less offensive way of adults telling us to shut up. Of course, I never took it to be less offensive, it was just my assumption as to why it was used instead of the latter.

But I always felt offended; thought of as less of a person. In fact, the idea that adults thought they were being savvy by saying, "Kids should be seen and not heard," rather than cutting me off mid-sentence with a "Zip it!" was even more insulting. It was as if they thought I wasn't smart enough to know they were humoring themselves thinking they'd pulled a fast one over on a kid. But not only was I smart enough to know, I was jaded enough to think to myself, *Okay, fine. Go f*ck yourself then.*

That edginess in me grew stronger over time. It ballooned into a hatred, an anger, and a chip on my shoulder too big to carry. When you grow up with negativity, I guess it's no surprise that you evolve into negativity. But what did surprise me was how impactful that phrase became to my adult voice. It wasn't until I was years into therapy for my anxiety and depression, that I realized that one saying had become my approach to so many situations: I was to be seen and not heard.

Whether it was a question I had in the classroom, a concern I had at work, or the fear I felt while being sexually assaulted on the floor of my best friend's dorm room in college, speaking up was something I didn't know how to do; I just couldn't bring myself to do it.

Finding my voice is something I've had to work on, intentionally, for decades. I'm a people pleaser; I prioritize the thoughts and feelings of others over my own. I spent years sacrificing my comfort and forgoing my own struggles to keep the peace. But there is no stronger weapon at your disposal than your voice. Thoughts and feelings can be powerful, but they are even more so when you can give a voice to them.

In *Fighting Your Inner Voice*, my first publication with Code Breaker Inc., I discussed the importance of verbalizing your thoughts and feelings. Your inner thoughts, I explained, are like a bully, torturing you from the inside out. But much like with a bully, the way you make the harassment stop, is by fighting back. That fight is your voice.

When you verbalize what you're feeling, you take away the one thing that lets your bully thrive: the isolation. This is why voice is so important to every individual. This is why we have to encourage people, students and staff alike, to use their voice, say what they feel. Doing so is healthy, empowering, and productive; for the individuals doing it and for those who get to see it happening.

But there's an interesting thing about voice; something we often misunderstand in education. Voice isn't just verbal. Students don't have to speak to say something. Voice is about communication; connection. Voice can be visual, it can be kinesthetic. Voice can be written, it can even be silent.

There have been many studies conducted on communication. Not all of them have come to the same results, but a majority of researchers and experts agree that anywhere from 70–90% of communication is nonverbal. Of course nonverbal communication doesn't work if educators aren't perceptive. We have to *want* to give students a voice in order for them to effectively use theirs.

I taught Advanced Placement Biology for years. Many of the students with whom I worked were high achieving students with a lot of pressure on them to succeed; real or imagined. When my students tested, I paid particular attention to their body language and behaviors. One student in particular, I noticed would aggressively shake his leg whenever he took a test. At the end of class one day, as he turned in his exam, I asked him, "Hey, Bryan, do you have anxiety, or get particularly anxious when you take tests?" Bryan was shocked by my question.

"Yeah, I do actually. How did you know?"

"I saw you bouncing your leg during the test today. I've actually noticed it before."

"Yeah, I do that because I'm anxious," Bryan confirmed.

"Hence, the question. I have anxiety, too. Let's talk about what we can do to make you less anxious for tests. You're a really smart kid, there is no reason why you should be out thinking yourself."

"I do that, right?!" Bryan seemed relieved someone was finally understanding him.

"You do. And we can work on it."

I spent time before each of the next tests working with Bryan one-on-one to help him review content. We worked on essays together in class, went back over test questions he'd gotten wrong previously, and dove deeper into the concepts with which he wasn't as confident. Bryan went from an anxious test taker with a ton of potential, to a high achieving student who earned a qualifying score on his College Board Advanced Placement exam. The trigger for his success was not just his own voice, but his teacher's ability to *listen* to what he was *saying*.

We've heard it a million times: the foundation of education is building positive personal relationships with students. Think about any one of the highly functional relationships you've ever been in. Did you have a voice in that relationship? Did you feel heard? Was the other person attuned to you enough to hear your voice even when you couldn't? If the relationship was successful, then the answer to all of those questions was "Yes." One-sided relationships never work. People need to feel valued in a relationship to want to stay. One of the most impactful ways you can show someone they are valued is by listening to them; seeing their voice, hearing their voice.

Speaking up can be scary. It's frightening to put your voice out there because every time you do, you risk facing rejection; rejection of your opinion, of your thought, or even of your presence. But what we should be instilling in young people is that voice isn't about the specifics of the message they are trying to relay. Rather, it's about the tone and tenor of their voice; the approach. This, of course, is a much more advanced lesson to the concept of voice. Unfortunately, too many educators jump to this lesson first. Instead of celebrating students for using their voices, we scold them for being too loud, too disruptive, or too disrespectful.

Start small. Celebrate with students for simply speaking up, no matter how they do so. From there, ask questions; be the direction students will need to communicate their thoughts and emotions effectively. Explain to them that their voice has an impact regardless of their intent. And finally, be consistent. The more a student does something, the better they will get at it. Continue to guide their voice to get to the root of what they are trying to say. The more questions you ask and the more committed you are to their voice, the more comfortable, and better they will get at using it. Because the lesson I should have been taught when I was a kid was not that kids should be seen and not heard, but rather, it's not what you have to say, it's how you say it.

1100 1011

"Technology gives all my students a voice," I wrote in my first course as a University Instructor.

I had been hired to teach three sections of Integration of Information and Computer Technology at the local university's Faculty of Education. This was an opportunity I could not let pass me by. After all, I was the king of technology integration.

Early in my career, technology played a minor role in my classroom even though I thought it was everything. It wasn't until I truly evaluated whether or not the technology was improving learning or just a substitute for something else, that I began to dissect its role.

At one time, technology was an event. In the early days of my teaching career I would sign out the computer lab on a Friday afternoon and march my class down to the hottest space in school. And I don't mean *the place to be*, I mean *temperature*. I would assign my students the same mundane computer task and tell myself I was integrating technology.

In some ways I was. At the time not every student had a computer at home. I suppose this still remains true. I figured that being exposed to the computer was the most important facet of this learning opportunity. But what I didn't realize was that I was quieting certain students. Some of them were intimidated by the machine as they had little experience with it. They didn't want to stand out as the "have nots."

Technology integration should focus on making the lesson better, not using the technology because it is flashy. In my classroom, technology was another tool in the belt. And the bigger the tool belt, the more voices I heard.

Minecraft and coding were game changers in my classroom with regards to students with autism. These tools allowed them to share their thoughts in nonverbal ways. Students identified with learning disabilities found themselves enthralled in their own creative technological spaces, both physically with hardware and digitally with programs. Many of these students were creating games and apps, and much like my lawn mower story, my job was to identify curriculum in everything they did.

Suddenly the quiet students had a voice and the louder students began hollering at me, metaphorically, through content creation. At one time I used to call on the first student who raised their hand in order to keep the discussion moving. What I now realize is that I never gave everyone an equal opportunity to even process what I was saying and consider their own answers. I was focused on speed and accuracy, which was terribly inequitable. Technology changed everything as I learned that time cannot be the same constant for all.

But perhaps the biggest shift in our school's culture came after our first annual student-lead TEDx Talk event. While we practiced the talks with our students, we never polished their words or changed what they had to say. After all, this was the goal. This was the beginning of a movement. This started the drastically needed change in our school's culture. This was the real deal, and it was raw and honest. And man, those young kids did a stellar job sharing their thoughts in such a profound manner.

"You tell me what to draw in art class and grade my creativity based on how well it looks compared to someone else's. I just want to be creative, and that cannot be standardized." Powerful words. Said by a 13 year old.

Our student-lead TEDx Talk event screamed volumes to the community. I mean the *entire* community. Staff, students, parents. All stakeholders were listening. This wasn't a checklist or Google Form asking kids about their interests. This was us asking them to be real.

"If you'll say it online to a peer, we want to hear about it." That was the underlying motto.

Many adults were apprehensive. Many staff members were concerned. Would students use this platform to speak too truthfully? Would they attack the character of others in the building? Of course not. We gave them an opportunity to make genuine change. There was no way they would jeopardize that. This was their moment. This was their Woodstock. This event encapsulated a student body generation and we were ready to listen to what needed to be said.

I remember thinking that the issues that were being brought up were systemic and while not all directly related to our school, it made me realize that we had a responsibility to do better. We could change the system as a team. This is the power of synergy.

When I step back and unravel this experience, a few criteria come to mind. For starters, we needed an administrative team prepared to be called to action by the student body. We needed to keep an open mind and recognize that many issues coming to light were not about us, the adults, personally. Most of the issues stemmed from the dictation of what these students had to learn. There was a common theme of 21st century learning and being connected but our students felt they were being exposed to 19th century ideologies at school.

For me, this is the pure definition of leadership. My administrator sat in the front row and nodded along. He acknowledged every word that every student speaker said as evidenced in his body language and he looked every speaker in the eye. He didn't take notes, and he didn't have to. There was an overarching theme: by definition, school needed to change.

This leader would also randomly appear in our classrooms, offer to take over and tell us to go watch a colleague teach. I felt my voice heard as much as my students'.

We knew we had an obligation to amplify these messages. If our student body agreed with the overall messaging, the larger community needed to hear it. We selected the most impactful talks and invited the district trustees and higher ups for a second show. With some extra confidence, these student speakers absolutely crushed the second sold out show.

Soon the media caught wind.

This was a legitimate movement.

This was change.

This was growth.

In a world that changes overnight, the only strategy guaranteed to fail is *not* trying something new. School, not necessarily education, often becomes a place of preparation for what's next, and quite often, what's *next* is more school.

We cannot prepare students for a future we haven't experienced yet, a world with tools that have yet to be invented, and problems we do not yet know are problematic. We should be expected to attempt to develop skills of problem solving, creativity, and critical thinking so students can adapt to any changing variables tossed at them into their adult lives.

From an incredibly large lens, technology not only gives all students a voice, it allows us to explore. And by human definition, we are explorers. We've explored this planet and are starting to explore our universe further. What makes student voice and technology integration so crucial to our existence, is the continual sharing of ideas. In recent times, this concept of idea sharing has gone viral. It has become exponential.

The further we explore the ideas of our students and listen to their voices, the further we can explore the universe as one connected human species. That one quiet kid in the back of our classroom might be the one piloting the next NASA space shuttle, but only if we are willing to listen.

CONCLUSION

Like many systems, education is a long standing institution filled with rules, regulations, and policies that have been in place since schooling began. Systems require parameters in order to function properly. How we conceptualize *function* is what makes all the difference. What is the purpose of education? Better yet, what is the purpose of school? These rules, regulations, and policies filter their way down into schools and land firmly at the classroom level. They shape our classrooms, our programs, and ultimately our students. Even with the best intentions, they can provide a great deal of harm as they have been generated with a one size fits all formula as per the confines of the system. These protocols have immense power and influence and can generate educators who feel they are just cogs on a wheel of the status quo. Round and round we go, like hamsters, running full speed from the first day of school until the last.

Disruptors might start as solo venturers, but they'll soon be accompanied by more people, real people, perfectly imperfect people; the best kind there is. These people help reduce learning phobia and treat students as humans, not test scores. But it starts with us. We have to challenge the norm and sometimes this means taking the heat or standing alone on an idea that we know is best for those we serve. Taking these risks and making change can make people see us as disruptive. But as educators, we are faced with the challenge of meeting the individual needs of those we teach in a world that quite literally changes overnight. And so to meet the needs of all our learners, we must challenge the way things have always been done because growth requires change.

With that growth and change comes risk taking and failure. Creating change requires disruption; disruption of what it means to be an educator; disruption of what it means to be a leader; disruption of a system that defines failure as an end point to learning, not a beginning. For this change to occur, we must lean into failure as a means of learning, we must be comfortable with discomfort, and we must disrupt the status quo.

BRIAN ASPINALL

Brian Aspinall is an educator and best selling author and is considered one of the brightest STEM innovators in education. He is the founder of Code Breaker Inc., an organization whose mission is to engage students and amplify voices of passionate educators who believe that all students can achieve if given a fair chance. He travels the globe speaking and leading professional development programs that inspire educators to create curious seeking individuals in classrooms built on a community of trust, risk-taking and a freedom to fail. His first book, *Code Breaker*, continues to top the charts in STEM education with a focus on rethinking assessment and evaluation. He was awarded the Prime Minister's Award for Teaching Excellence for his work with coding and computational thinking. His enthusiasm, thought leadership, and approach to building capacity within STEM education has made him a sought after speaker across the globe.

DAPHNE MCMENEMY

Daphne McMenemy is an educator, author and speaker. Her first book, Gracie, is based on her personal experiences in the classroom. Gracie is a young girl whose learning is brought to life when her teacher introduces her to coding and a new way of thinking. As a child and young adult, Daphne was focused on becoming an educator with purpose, to improve the lives of her students and make an impact on their

educational journey. As an educator for the past 18 years, she has created opportunity for children in her classroom to explore learning in innovative ways. Using STEM to engage children as young as kindergarten age in discovering learning through coding, she develops numeracy, literacy and computational thinking skills through creative exploration. Her experience in the classroom has proven to support even the most hesitant learners in building confidence in their abilities and engaging in the learning process. Daphne is committed to building relationships, meeting students where they are, appreciating each individual, and finding opportunity to engage and motivate students in creative, innovative ways. Her newest venture allows her an extensive creative outlet as Managing Director of Code Breaker Inc.

MATTHEW X. JOSEPH

Author of Power of Connections (Code Breaker Inc.), Stronger Together (X-Factor) Modern Mentor, Reimagining Mentorship in Education (Times 10 Publications), Dr. Matthew X. Joseph has been a school and district leader in many capacities in public education over his 27 years in the field. Experiences such as Executive Director for Teaching and Learning, the Director of Curriculum and Instruction, Director of Digital Learning and Innovation, elementary school principal, classroom teacher, and district professional development specialist have provided Matt's incredible insights on how to best support teaching and learning and led to nationally published articles and opportunities to speak at multiple state and national events. His master's degree is in special education and his Ed.D. in Educational Leadership from Boston College. Matt is the CEO of X-Factor EDU. X-Factor EDU is a full-service professional development organization with educators from multiple countries and backgrounds. In addition to publishing the voice of amazing educators, they provide leadership coaching, district consulting and workshops, and keynotes around many educational topics. Click here to learn more about the company. Matt is the president-elect of MASCD (The Massachusetts chapter of ASCD) and is recognized as one of 10 national leaders on the rise.

CHRISTINE RAVESI-WEINSTEIN

Christine Ravesi-Weinstein currently serves as a high school Assistant Principal in Massachusetts and previously worked as a high school science department chair for four years and classroom teacher for 15. Diagnosed with anxiety and depression at 23, Christine began her journey towards mental wellness. She began a non-profit organization in June of 2017 aimed at removing the stigma of mental illness and  promoting physical activity as a means to cope with anxiety. As an avid writer and educator, Christine became passionate about bridging the two with her advocacy for mental health. Since March of 2019, she has had numerous nationally published articles including the number one most read article of 2019 on *eSchool News*. She also had the number six and eight most read articles in that year.

Christine has presented at numerous national conferences including ASCD CEL 2019, Empower20 (selected), ASCD CTE 2020 (selected), the Tech & Learning 2020 Virtual Leadership Summit, the 2020 ASCD Virtual Conference, ESEA 2021 National Conference and has provided professional development for educators in various districts. Christine is an MASCD Board Member, and her first book, *Anxious*, was published in March 2020.

CODE BREAKER INC.

CONSULTING

To learn more about the authors
or to book them for a visit to your school, district, or event,
visit www.codebreakeredu.com

INSPIRE · INNOVATE

LEAD · TEACH · LEARN

CODE BREAKER LEADERSHIP SERIES

CODE BREAKER KID COLLECTION

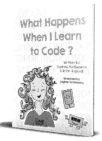
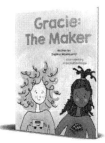

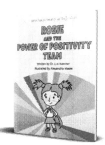

THE X FACTOR LIBRARY

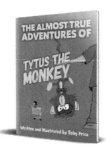

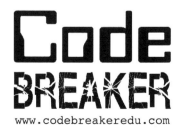